THE HAPPY

THE HAPPY WIZARD is a gently satirical fairy tale written for family entertainment; but it is a fairy story with a difference, being both traditional and unconventional. No attempt has been made to talk down to children, but neither are the doubles entendres tinged with blue.

The royal hero breaks with tradition in that he has the failings of an ordinary young man; the pretty heroine is a radical; the "baddie" is a not-unlikeable villain, and his opposite number, the fairy, is a graduate of a most unusual university! The adventures of these and other characters are slyly manipulated by a semi-retired wizard whose absent-minded magic produces unexpected results. Needless to say, there is a happy ending, but this too, has an unforeseen twist.

This is a complete acting edition containing all the moves and lighting, music, costume and property plots. There are comprehensive production notes which cover style of presentation and descriptions of all the characters. The melody lines of the simple songs are included in the book.

The play can be presented with six men and five women.

FOR C.E.

THE HAPPY WIZARD

a satirical fairy tale
in three acts

by

KATHLEEN EDLESTON

Music and Lyrics by KATHLEEN EDLESTON

HANBURY PLAYS
KEEPER'S LODGE
BROUGHTON GREEN
DROITWICH
WORCESTERSHIRE WR9 7EE

FIRST PUBLISHED 1973
by
C. COMBRIDGE LIMITED,
WRENTHAM STREET,
BIRMINGHAM B5 6QT

© Copyright 1972 K. Edleston

Printed by Stationery Print Ltd. Worcester, England

**Essex County
Council Libraries**

This play, music and lyrics are fully protected by copyright and are subject to the payment of a royalty.

All enquiries concerning the rights for professional or amateur stage performances should be addressed to the publishers, SAMUEL FRENCH LTD.

FOR PERFORMING RIGHTS
APPLY:-
SAMUEL FRENCH LTD.
52 FITZROY STREET
LONDON W1P 6JR

This play is available for performance either with or without music. But neither the play nor its songs and music may be performed unless prior permission has been obtained from the publishers. It is advisable to complete an application form—obtainable from the publishers—before rehearsals commence.

No performance of this play or of extracts from the play may be given unless permission has been obtained in advance.

It is an infringement of the copyright to copy any part of this play by manuscript, typescript, photography or by any other means of reproduction.

SONGS

Music and lyrics by Kathleen Edleston.
Musical arrangements by Sheila Corbett.

ACT I

Back in the Book (Felix, Augustus, Penelope and Hilarius).
Dreaming Dreams (Sally).
Back in the Book. Reprise. (Felix, Augustus, Penelope and Hilarius).
The Mixture (Hilarius).
Giddy-yup Nelly (Penelope).

ACT II

Breath of Fresh Air (Felix).
No Happy Ending (Sally).

ACT III

If I Could Write Music (Felix).
Happy Ending (The Company) (Reprise of the melody 'No Happy Ending').
Back in the Book (Hilarius).

Characters in the play (in order of appearance).

FELIX	King of Mythuania
THE ARCHDUKE AUGUSTUS	his companion
HILARIUS	a wizard
DISCORD	a likeable demon
PENELOPE BUNN	a countrywoman
DEWDROP	an unusual fairy
DAFFY-DOWN-DILLY	a not so simple village maiden
BILLY PIPPIN	a yokel
SALLY LUNN	Penelope's niece
NELLY	a nightmare
DR. SOLFA	custodian of the Realm of Music
MISS MELODY	his personal assistant

A Herald of the Royal Household.
Villagers and inhabitants of the Realm of Music.

SCENES

ACT I

Scene 1. The Story Book Opens—early one morning.
Scene 2. The Village Green in Little Woody Bottom in Pantomania—mid afternoon.

ACT II

Scene 1. The Land of Legend—after sunset.

ACT III

Scene 1. The Realm of Music—six days later.
Scene 2. The Story Book Closes.

THE HAPPY WIZARD was first presented at the CRESCENT THEATRE, Birmingham, on January 9th, 1956, with the following cast:—

FELIX	Eric Latimer
AUGUSTUS	George Cranage
HILARIUS	Bill Reid
DISCORD	Alec Dawkins
PENELOPE BUNN	Peggy Hughes
JOY	Jane Biddle
BILLY PIPPIN	Charles Cruxton
DAFFY	Kitty Bristow
SALLY LUNN	Alice Wood
DR. SOLFA	Kenneth Cope
MISS MELODY	Joyce Lewis
NELLY	Kenneth Cope and Joyce Lewis

Other parts played by Charles Cruxton and Muriel Yarwood.
    Production by Vernon Wood and John Taylor.
    Set designed by Eric Latimer.
    Stage manager Peter Richards.
    Costumes designed by Eric Latimer.
    Musical arrangements by John Taylor and Dominic Cain.
    Pianist—Leslie Holland.

Lighting Cue 1
Music Cue 1 (Overture)
Lighting Cue 2

ACT I

Scene 1

    The first set occupies one third of the stage depth and consists of a painted backing representing a row of outsize books supported between giant book-ends. Behind this a traverse curtain of some dark material conceals the second set. The books, with one exception, are in the conventional position and titles of well known fairy stories are painted on the spines. The centre book is at a right angle to the others and the brightly painted cover showing its title "The Happy Wizard" faces the audience. This cover is a practical door. Immediately behind this door is a light wooden frame over which is stretched white paper to indicate the fly-leaf. This paper has to be renewed for each performance. There are two stacks of books lying flat to serve as seats down stage R. and L.

    As the curtain opens the cover is seen to move slightly as if pushed from within. Suddenly it bursts open and Felix springs through the fly-leaf like a circus performer leaping through a paper hoop. He is young, handsome and gorgeously attired in a costume of the "fairy tale mediaeval" period as befits a hero of royal birth . . . it should be emphasised however that this part should not be played as a principal boy.

Music Cue 2
Lighting Cue 3

Felix: I'm free! At last I'm free to breathe and talk and move. So this is the outside world; it looks exciting. (*Turns back to book*). Come out, Augustus. Freedom is wonderful.
Augustus: (*from within*). Your Majesty, is it safe to proceed?
Felix: How do I know? But who cares? Safety is dull and danger is exhilarating. Do hurry up and don't be such a lily livered old coward.
    (*Augustus emerges cautiously. In contrast to Felix he is a small man, middle aged, soberly dressed, pedantic of speech and prim of manner*).

ACT ONE   THE HAPPY WIZARD

Lighting Cue 4

Augustus: What a strange place! I like it not.

Felix: Stop moaning and thank your lucky stars you are now three dimensional rather than squashed flat between the pages of a book which no one has yet read. If we hadn't used our initiative we might have stayed on that shelf for years, doomed to oblivion.

Augustus: Sire, this escapade does not meet with my approval. And when Her Majesty the Queen Mother (*bows reverently at the mention of this intimidating lady's name*) hears of it heads will roll like ninepins, including mine.

Felix: Nonsense! I rule my own kingdom, no matter what my mother thinks. But we are on holiday now and ready for adventures.

Augustus: Adventures! Nasty dangerous things. I strongly advise returning to page one without undue delay. (*Turns purposefully towards book*).

Felix: (*taking his arm*). I won't hear of it. Surely you want to find out what happens to us and if no one is going to turn the pages then we must do it ourselves.

Augustus: (*aside*). I see that I shall have to humour my young master. (*To Felix*). Your Majesty, let us look at the final page, then, with our curiosity satisfied, we can return to the beginning without further ado.

Felix: I am surprised at you, trying to cheat like a romantic old maid with a library book. I refuse to consider it. (*Takes a pace down stage R*). All we know at present is that once upon a time you and I set out from the palace on a long journey. That's an intriguing situation and I want to know where we were going and why, and until we do something positive we shall never know what's on page two.

Augustus: Sire, as your former tutor, now elevated to the position of royal amanuensis I feel it my bounden duty to point out the perils we may encounter in this strange outside world.

Felix: Adventure! Augustus. That's the sole object of the project.

Augustus: Tut! tut! Such a headstrong attitude becomes not a reigning monarch. Are you not aware of your responsibilities to the people? It is high time you thought of marriage and only yesterday your royal mother (*bows*)

Felix:	ordered me to prepare a list of eligible princesses from which you are to choose a royal bride. (*walking away from him*) I am not yet ready to consider marriage. I want to see the world and sow a few wild oats before I have to settle down.
Augustus:	If your Majesty wishes to study agriculture, a term at one of the country colleges could be arranged.
Felix:	No young man needs instruction in sowing wild oats —it's instinctive!
Augustus:	(*aside*) Dear me, I shall have to play along with His Majesty for a while until he gets this foolish idea out of his system. (*Turns to Felix*) Your Majesty, I have a plan. Let us have just one little adventure in which you rescue a princess, one on the approved list of course, from a dreadful monster and . . . .
Felix:	(*slapping him on the back*) Good old Augustus! That's just the very thing I want to do. I knew you wouldn't let me down. Let's get started right away. (*Pause*) Oh, but there's a snag. What do we do with the princess after I've rescued her?
Augustus:	Tradition has it that you marry her, Sire.
Felix:	Am I to understand that I'm to be allowed just one little adventure ending in marriage to some milk and water princess, and then be forced to spend the rest of my days living happily ever after, raising strings of pimply princes and podgy princesses? It's not on, Augustus, it's just not on.
Augustus:	It would be necessary to have only two or three progeny to ensure the succession . . . .
Felix:	Devil take the succession!
Discord:	(*offstage*) Thank you. I will. (*Peal of diabolical laughter*).
Augustus:	What was that? I pray you, Sire, let us go back to the palace before it is too late.
Felix:	Do stop behaving like a frightened hen and let us decide on a plan of action. But first I want you to take on yet another royal appointment. (*Takes up a regal stance*). In order to preserve our liberty, all fights and duels in connection with our proposed adventures must be on a strictly business footing, and from now on you are appointed as our agent. We wish to make it known that before we dispose of any

ACT ONE THE HAPPY WIZARD

dragon, monster or giant it is to be written into our contract that any maiden be she princess or peasant, incidentally rescued is to receive but a farewell kiss or a gallant wave, according to her social standing. In our opinion girls are a nuisance and we will not have our life cluttered up with the female of the species. Is that understood?

Augustus: (*Sadly*) I comprehend the position Your Majesty.
Felix: Good. Now let's make a start. Did you remember to bring along a map and compass?
Augustus: Your Majesty is forgetting I had only five minutes' notice of this expedition.
Felix: Of course. I did rather spring this on you, but had I given you warning of my plan no doubt you and my royal mother would have thought of some way of preventing my escape.
Augustus: Indeed Your Majesty tends to misjudge my good intentions . . . .
Felix: Come off it Augustus, you know perfectly well you would.

Sound Effects Cues 1 and 2

Augustus: Come off it indeed! This constant descent into the vernacular of the proletariat ill becomes one of such exalted rank. The Queen Mother (*bows*) would no doubt . . . . (*he breaks off and sniffs as little plumes of smoke begins curling round the edges of the book and a roaring noise is heard in the distance*).

Lighting Cue 5

Felix: Look! Smoke! And roaring noises! It can only be a dragon. Hold my cloak. (*He flings it off and drops it over Augustus' head. Felix draws his sword and prepares to advance practising sword play as he goes*).
Augustus: (*struggling with cloak*) Do not apprehend it, Sire. Let us take cover while we may. (*Felix shakes off Augustus' detaining hand*). I haven't had time to draw up the contract containing the clause about the maiden.
Felix: Too late now! And this opportunity is too good to miss. Girls can't stand the sight of blood and she is sure to faint when the fighting starts. When I've

dealt with the dragon you stand by ready to help me make a quick getaway before she has time to regain consciouness.

(*Augustus retreats downstage R and cowers unsuccessfully trying to hide behind the small pile of books while Felix advances towards the now visibly shaking book cover. The king is almost knocked flying by Hilarius as he steps out of the book. The latter is tall, bewhiskered and bespectacled; his dark blue robe is patterned with silver stars and moons; he is the conventional story book wizard apart from his head gear. This is a black bowler hat and he carries a neatly rolled black umbrella. The smoke and noise die away*).

Sound Effects Cues 3 and 4

Hilarius: Sir, may I ask why you were about to attack my pet dragon?

Lighting Cue 6

Felix: (*indignantly*) Your pet dragon? Are you telling me that ferocious rip-roaring animal is a pet?
Hilarius: But he was only roaring with laughter — he's never seen anyone quite like you and your friend before.
Felix: Then he's a very ill-mannered beast. And his fiery breath is more than a little unpleasant.
Hilarius: Oh dear! He must have been eating the pickled onions again. In future I shall see that he has pickled jumpers instead.
Felix: Pickled jumpers?
Hilarius: Oh mearie dee, no dearie me. I mean pickled jerkins.
Augustus: (*coming out of hiding*) Pickled gherkins. I repeat —pickled gherkins.
Hilarius: Thank you, kind sir. Do forgive me, gentlemen. I am apt to get a little muddled at times and I forget things. My age, you know.
Felix: And we are forgetting our manners. Allow me to introduce myself—I am Felix Rex and this gentleman is my travelling companion, Augustus Dukes.
Augustus: But Your Maje . . . .
Felix: (*quietly to Augustus*) Quiet, my friend. We had better travel incognito, it may save complications.
Hilarius: I am Hilarius, a wizard by profession, semi-retired.

ACT ONE　　　　THE HAPPY WIZARD

Augustus: If you are indeed a wizard, where is your steeple hat?
Hilarius: *(feels hat)* Oh dear, oh dear! *(Takes it off and examines it)* This appears to be my brother's hat. But why am I wearing it? Ah, now I remember. I must have picked it up by mistake when I saw him off at the air terminal this morning.
Felix: Then your brother is not a wizard?
Hilarius: Indeed he is. He is a most brilliant financial wizard. This morning he was off to stay with some gnome friends in er, Zurich, yes, that's the name of the place. He will be so embarrassed having to wear my hat with his Saville Row suit. I must hurry home and post his bowler and brolly off to Switzerland right away. *(Turns, then stops abruptly).* Oh dear! I am a wim ditted old wizard; I quite forgot, I can't go home, that is, not until I've found my kingdom.
Augustus: *(obviously bored, he walks down stage)* Have you lost your kingdom?
Felix: *(interested)* How did it happen? In battle?
Hilarius: Oh, dear me, no. I went out to have a cup of coffee with a goblin and when I came back it wasn't there.
Felix: But you can't mislay a kingdom like an umbrella or a library book.
Hilarius: *(goes over to Felix)* It isn't like a library book, not at all; it's quite a different shape. *(Confidentially)* Let me tell you about it. I suppose it's really all my own fault for I stayed away much longer than I intended, but I was having such an enjoyable time hobnobbing with this gobhoblin, no, gobnogging with the bobhoblin, no, bobnobbing with . . . .
Augustus: *(sinking onto pile of books, resigned to being bored).* Hobnobbing with the hobgoblin.
Hilarius: Thank you sir. As I was saying, I was a little late returning. In fact I was too late, for my kingdom had vanished.
Augustus: My dear Wizard, there is a perfectly logical explanation. After leaving your friend you took the wrong turning on the way home with the obvious result that you are lost in strange territory. But if you will inform me of the latitude and longitude of your domain I will endeavour, with the aid of the sun, to calculate its geographical location in relation to your present position.

THE HAPPY WIZARD — ACT ONE

Hilarius: How very kind. But what you ask is impossible. You see, my kingdom is abstract. Sometimes it's here, sometimes it's there, occasionally it is everywhere and at the moment it's nowhere at all. Isn't it sad?

Augustus: (*goes up to Felix*). Sire . . . .

Felix: Felix! Remember!

Augustus: (*quietly*) Sir, the gentleman is obviously mad and we must humour him. I will think up some excuse and we will be on our way.

(*Hilarius wanders about as if looking for something*).

Felix: (*to Augustus*) Certainly not. I forbid you to interfere. I like this old boy and the situation is certainly interesting. Tell me, Hilarius, is this the first time you have lost your kingdom?

Hilarius: (*coming over to Felix*) Regrettably no. But as a general rule I have managed to find it again fairly quickly, but this time however I fear it is gone for good. Oh dear, oh dear! The Spirit of Joy will be so annoyed. I have betrayed her trust in me.

Felix: The Spirit of Joy? Who is she?

Hilarius: A sort of fairy.

Augustus: Fairies! Pah! They are merely mythical characters in story books.

Felix: Augustus, you surprise me, you really do. (*Pointing to book*) Have you forgotten so soon?

Augustus: (*sniffs and ignores the jibe*) Venerable wizard, can you not be a little more explicit?

Hilarius: (*sitting down on books down stage R*). Long, long ago when the world was very young the Spirit of Joy and the Demon Discord quarrelled over the possession of the Kingdom of Harmony. Joy, being a sort of female fairy had the last word and took over the kingdom. She appointed me Governor General, in sole charge. And now I've lost it she will never forgive me. I fear Discord is behind this for he is determined to get it back by crook or by hook. Oh dear! I'm such a willy old sizzard, no silly old wizard. How could I have been so careless?

Felix: What an intriguing story! But do not despair for Augustus and I will help you find your kingdom. This Discord now, he sounds a villainous type and I cannot wait to get to grips with him. Where is he to be found?

ACT ONE THE HAPPY WIZARD

Lighting Cue 7   Sound Effects Cue 5

(*There is a flash of lightning and a crash of thunder and Discord, a tall, well built figure dressed in glittering green and black stands up stage L*).

Discord: Ho, ho! My pretty popinjay! Those are rash words. Take care you do not have cause to regret them.

Felix: Demon Discord, I presume? I would have you know, sir, that I do not care to be called a pretty popinjay. (*unsheathes sword*).

Discord: Do not trouble to draw your sword, it would crumble to dust if I but touched it.

Felix: I am not afraid.

Augustus: (*cowering behind Hilarius*). I am!

Discord: (*to Felix*) I like your courage, young sir. It would be a pity to kill one so young. Instead I have another plan. I will make you an offer, a wager.

Felix: I accept.

Augustus: (*creeping out from behind Hilarius*) Tarry a moment. You cannot guess what this may entail. And, moreover, the Queen Mother (*bows*) does not approve of gambling.

Discord: Be silent, pedagogue! (*Augustus retreats*). (*Discord turns to Felix*) Now, young jackanapes. This is my proposition. Listen carefully. Should you succeed in finding the Kingdom of Harmony within seven days you and your egghead friend may come or go as you please, but should you fail . . . .

Felix: Yes?

Discord: You must marry the first woman whom you encounter after I have taken my departure.

Felix: But this is diabolical. I have no time for women.

Discord: Precisely. But you have already accepted my challenge. Do you wish to withdraw?

Felix: You insult me, sir. I am a man of honour. I have promised Hilarius I would find his kingdom and I intend to keep my word.

Discord: We shall see. I recognise a worthy foe despite your dandified dress. But may I remind you that there is but one week in which to complete your impossible task. You cannot succeed, and at the seventh hour of the seventh day I shall see you married to your predestined bride, the future queen of Mythuania. (*Laughs*).

Felix: But you know who I am! My companion and I are travelling incognito.
Discord: Incognito? And wearing the royal crown of Mythuania? Really King Felix, you will have to do better than that if you are to win the wager. Farewell! But I will be back! (*Goes out L. Lightning and thunder flash*).

Lighting Cue 8   Sound Effects Cue 6

Felix: Augustus, why did you not tell me to remove my crown?
Augustus: It is not for me to give such an order, Your Majesty. Your Royal Mother (*bows*) would not tolerate such behaviour.
Felix: My mother is not here. And she ceased to be regent four years ago when I came of age; a fact which you seem determined to ignore.
Hilarius: (*coming between them*) Gentlemen, no arguments please. Had we not better start looking for Harmony? Time is rushing by.
Felix: And we must not waste it. But tell me, Hilarius, how did Discord know I dislike women? Or was his idea of a punishment just coincidence?
Hilarius: He knows many things. His espionage system is excellent and he is a master of disguise.
Augustus: The situation might be worse, for even if you do have to marry the first woman we encounter, she may be quite presentable. Then we can return to the palace in triumph. The Queen Mother (*bows*) will have a daughter in law and my head will be safe.
Felix: Stop worrying about your silly head! You know my mother's bark is far worse than her bite. She will probably just banish you to the salt mines. I'm the one with the real problem.
Hilarius: Pardon me, gentlemen. I know I'm only a silly old wizard, but can we not start looking now?
Felix: Right. Where shall we start? Where do you suggest we look?
Augustus: (*with a superior air*) In the book, of course.
Hilarius: Now why didn't I think of that? But one moment, kind sirs. (*To Felix*) I think it might be better if you were to remove your crown; we do not wish to attract the attention of outdits and bandlaws.

ACT ONE　　　THE HAPPY WIZARD

Augustus: Bandits and outlaws!
Felix: (*removes crown and gives it to Augustus*) Take care of this for the time being. We will stop at the first post office on the way and you can send it back to the palace, registered, of course. You may enclose a note stating it is on my orders if you are afraid of my mother's reaction. (*Augustus takes crown and puts it under his cloak*).

Music Cue 3

Hilarius: Now gentlemen, if we are quite ready I will look in the book. (*As he goes towards it the first few bars of the introductory music to the song are heard. Augustus and Felix follow and between verses they execute a few simple dance steps*).

Music Cue 4　　Lighting Cue 9

BACK IN THE BOOK

All: Back in the book,
That's where we'll look,
We must find the kingdom by hook or by crook.
We'll make a snook
At any spook
And fight ev'ry bandit and bashi-bazouk.
Tra la lalalalah.
Tra lalalalah lalalalalah.

(*At this point Hilarius opens the book and out tumbles Penelope Bunn. She is a jolly little country woman, round as a barrel with rosy cheeks and a turned up nose. Her cotton dress is bright, her wimple and apron spotless. She speaks with a slight 'mummerset' accent*).

Lighting Cue 10

Felix: What have you done?
The curse has begun,
I can't wed a woman who weighs half a ton.
See what I've won,
I am undone,
'Tis too much to hope that she might be a nun.

All: Tra la la etc.

Augustus: Oh sir, egad!
This is too bad,
How can we succeed in one short hebdobad?
She's no dryad
And this poor lad
Will end up a martyr in our Iliad.

All: Tra la la etc.

Penny: What's this about?
I may be stout
But I'm neither a nun nor a silly old trout!
Plain and homespun,
I am good fun,
Kind gentlemen all I'm Penelope Bunn.

All: Tra la la etc.

Felix: Please put her back,
I'm on the rack,
I can't love a woman who looks like a sack.
I am afraid,
Come to my aid,
For how can I marry this frightful old maid?

All: Tra la la etc.

Hilarius: Awful ambsace,
I'm in disgrace,
I can't put her back 'cause I can't find the place!

All: He's in disgrace,
Awful ambsace,
He can't put her back 'cause he can't find the place!
Tra la la etc.

Felix: Here's a fine how-do-you-do. Hilarius, I hope you realise just what this means in view of my commitments to Discord.

Hilarius: Indeed I do and I am most dreadfully sorry. But if the worst comes to the worst, if you know what I mean, she isn't such a frightful old attle baxe, is she. Couldn't you . . .

Felix: (*wearily*). Battle axe. And I couldn't.

Augustus: (*crossing to Penny and bowing formally*). Madam, prithee tell me, where is your permanent residence?

Penny:	I live in the village of Little Woody Bottom in the province of Pantomania. My young niece Sally Lunn and I have a tea garden. But you will be seeing it for yourselves when we get to chapter five.
Augustus:	I see. (*Turns to the others*). I fear there is nothing to be done but to take her with us until we reach the appropriate page from whence she came, that village with the vulgar appellation.
Hilarius:	We can do no less.
Felix:	I could well do without this complication.
Penny:	(*to Augustus*). I don't want to be no trouble good sir, but may I know your names? My mother always told me never to talk to strangers.
Augustus:	I am Augustus—er—Dukes.
Penny:	Mr. Dukes. I knew you be a gentleman the moment I set eyes on you.
Augustus:	Are you by any chance related to the well known Somerset family the Bath Buns?
Penny:	No, I don't think so, sir. But in my young days I used to be a member of the Chelsea set.
Felix:	(*impatiently*). Do stop wasting time, Augustus. There isn't a moment to lose—if I fail, you know the consequences.
Augustus:	(*brightly*). Have you considered the possibility that the lady may be already enchained in the bonds of matrimony?
Felix:	That would be too much to hope for. But I'll find out. (*To Penny*). Madam, have I the honour of addressing Miss or Mrs. Bunn?
Penny:	Alas! I be not married, but I have my memories—and my hopes.
Felix:	(*confused*). Please do not take my apparent show of interest too seriously. I only . . .
Augustus:	(*coming to the rescue*). Madam, I will acquaint you of the position. My companions and I are about to set out on a journey. As you are now our responsibility I am afraid you will have to accompany us until such time when we reach your domicile in Little Woody—er —Posterior.
Penny:	How kind you be to see me home. And perhaps I can be of help to you. It be a long way to Little Woody Bottom (*Augustus winces*) and you will be needing someone to cook your food and mend your clothes on the journey.

THE HAPPY WIZARD   ACT ONE

Felix: Do stop chattering, woman! (*Goes to Augustus*). Don't encourage her. She is already trying to trap one of us into a web of domesticity. We must take care. Hilarius, this journey is likely to be very arduous, in view of your years do you think you can make it?

Hilarius: But of course. I'm as mean as custard.

Augustus: As mean as custard?

Hilarius: No, you silly little man, you've got it the wrong way round—I'm as keen as mustard!

Felix: Be sensible, both of you. Now Hilarius, you are a wizard, haven't you got a magic carpet?

Hilarius: Unfortunately it's at home. But maybe I could borrow one from one of my eastern colleagues. Now let me see, there is Ping Pong in China or Ali in Afghanistan. It had better be Ali. Now where is my wand? Oh dear! I've only got my brother's brolly and all he seems to use it for is to conjure up bulls and bears in the market and that causes quite a lot of shocks and stares, I can assure you. I'm not sure that I can control it properly. Perhaps I can remember one of the magic phrases instead. Let me see. (*Chants*).
Hey diddle diddle and fiddle de dee,
Jumping jehosophat riddle me ree,
Adabra cadabra let's see what we'll see.

Lighting Cue 11

(*Discord appears left in the guise of an eastern merchant. He carries a large roll of carpet*).

Hilarius: Bumping jeans, no jumping beans! This is not Ali. Something must have gone wrong with the spell. My memory is getting very rusty.

Lighting Cue 12

Discord: Pray be not alarmed, oh my master. Ali is suffering from a surfeit of late Arabian nights and I have arranged to take his place during his indisposition.

Hilarius: But who are you?

Discord: I am Abdul from Baghdad.

Hilarius: How strange? I know of no one of that name in Dadbagh.

Penny: (*coming forward*). Sir, be you one of them there genies?

Discord: Lady of the rose-tipped nose, I am a Persian Djinn.

Penny: Then you do be one of them spirits that be found in bottles.

Felix: Be quiet Miss Penelope! Do not anger him, he may spirit us away to the mysterious east and you may find yourself a slave in the harem of a caliph. (*Aside*) Not a bad idea.

Discord: (*to Hilarius*). What do you require of me, oh wise master?

Hilarius: A magic carpet.

Discord: I knew it and I have here the very thing, oh master. (*He unrolls part of the roll of carpet leaving one end trailing off stage*). Note the exquisite workmanship, the patterns, the colours, the texture. It will outlast anyone's lifetime.

Felix: (*inspecting it*). It is a little narrow for our purpose.

Discord: Quality is better than quantity, noble son of a blue blooded father. My magic mat will soar like a swallow over the earth. There is nowhere in the universe it cannot fly.

Felix: (*to Augustus*) This fellow is much too plausible.

Hilarius: (*to Discord*). Would you be good enough to lend me the carpet for about a week?

Discord: (*grovelling*). But it is yours, my master. Accept it as a gift. You may be sure you may be taken for a ride, a wondrous ride! Farewell! (*Goes out chuckling*). (*Lightning flash and faint rumble of thunder*).

Lighting Cue 13   Sound Effects Cue 7

Augustus: Rather a hurried departure.

Hilarius: These eastern fellows are very busy. People are always rubbing lamps and rings and setting them impossible tasks. Climb aboard everybody.
(*They do so and settle down, Penny and Augustus both having difficulty in seating themselves comfortably*). Are we ready? One, two, three, Hey Presto! We're off! (*They are, as the carpet is pulled away from under them. Crestfallen they get to their feet*).
Oh dear! What a horrid trick.

Augustus: This incident needs reporting to the management of the magic circle.

Hilarius: Please don't do that. The last time a complaint was received the Magicians' Union called a strike. All the magicians downed wands and you just can't imagine the chaos it caused. Rabbits jumped out of hats and wouldn't go back; they ate up all the lettuce in the land.

Augustus: Master Felix, I told you we should not have left page one. This is a ghastly world, a place of greed and anarchy.
Felix: It is still preferable to the narrow confines of a royal palace and the stultifying feeling of being wrapped in royal cotton wool.
Augustus: But the Queen Mother (*bows*) maintains it is essential to wear wool next the skin.
Felix: Stuff and nonsense. I threw away my woolly vest when I came of age.
But now we must be practical. Hilarius, somewhile ago you mentioned a Spirit of Joy. Why not approach her for some help? Where does she live?
Hilarius: Nowhere. Yet anywhere. She's etherial. You can't see her, yet on certain occasions it is possible to feel her presence.
Felix: I think I understand.
Hilarius: (*crossing to him*). But I am quite sure you do not. I think that you think I am a little mad. But I'm not. I may be a wizzy old dizzard, no, a dizzy old wizard, but I do know what I am talking about—most of the time.
Penny: (*tugs Hilarius' sleeve and bobs a curtsy*). Please sir, couldn't we make do with an ordinary fairy like one of those that be at the bottom of my garden?
Hilarius: An excellent idea. Now why didn't I think of the District Fairy? She's always on call. Now let me see, the duty fairy for this area is Bell Blue. No, I am wrong, it's Blue Bell. (*He holds bowler hat to his ear and chants into handle of umbrella*).
Hello Blue Bell, can you hear?
Wizard calling, please come here.

Sound Effects Cue 8
(*There is a noise of 'number unobtainable'*).

Now what have I done wrong? Oh how silly of me, I had forgotten Blue Bell retired last year.
Felix: But fairies can't retire, they are immortal.
Hilarius: Of course they are. But we all grow older, and in middle age we take things more easily. By the time a fairy reaches forty she changes her occupation. The plump ones potter about in pantomime and the thin ones grace the tops of Christmas trees. And when they are really old, they go and live in the multi-storey flats

ACT ONE   THE HAPPY WIZARD

	for elderly fairies. If you look up in the sky on a dark night you can see all the little lights twinkling in the windows. Mortal men refer to these as stars and planets or some such newfangled rubbish, but then, they don't know any better.
Augustus:	An interesting but improbable theory. So now we do not have a district fairy?
Hilarius:	Oh yes we do, but she's a probationer. Now what's her name? Pear drop? Tear drop? Drop leaf? No that's a table. Dew-drop? That's it. She's a student fairy doing her post graduate preaching practice for her final diploma.
Felix:	Surely you mean teaching practice
Hilarius:	No. Preaching practice. Good fairies always preach.
Penny:	Please ask her to help us, Mr. Wizard. I be dying to get home for a cup of tea.
Hilarius:	(*again using hat and umbrella as an old fashioned telephone*). Come in Dewdrop, can you hear? Wizard calling, please come, dear.

Sound Effects Cue 9

(*There is a ringing tone followed by a few bars of 'harp music'*).

Dewdrop: Coming!

(*Dewdrop appears right. There is something a little unexpected about her appearance for although dressed in the conventional white tutu and tiara there is also a long college scarf wound round her neck and her eyes are partially obscured by large owl like spectacles. She carries a wand in one hand and a large black bag in the other*).

Hilarius: So sorry to have to call you out, my dear. Were you working on an urgent case?

Dewdrop: As it happens I was on my way to see you. Here is a special delivery from Zurich. (*Opens bag and takes out a steeple hat and rusty wand*). Sign please. (*Presents delivery sheet and pencil*).

Hilarius: My hat! (*Puts it on*). Thank you so much. I've been quite worried about it. Now would you be so kind as to take these to my young brother? (*Hands over bowler and brolly*).

Dewdrop: (*a little reluctantly*). Very well, but it means another detour. It's a bit of a nuisance for I was on my way to a fairy fly-in and this will make me late.
Augustus: Where was it you were going?
Dewdrop: To a fly-in round the wishing well. We student fairies are demonstrating against the public's habit of throwing their pennies down the well. I must be on my way.
Hilarius: Please wait a moment, dear Fairy Drop-out, no, Dewdrop, so sorry. Please help me find my lost Kingdom of Harmony.
Dewdrop: So you've mislaid it again? I was warned that this might happen, but frankly I don't think I've had sufficient experience to offer advice.
Felix: Then put us in touch with one of the fairy tutors. What about Joy, the spirit of Happiness?
Dewdrop: You must be joking. Joy only comes when unsought and stays but a short while.
Hilarius: (*to Felix*) You see what I meant about preaching practice? (*Felix nods*).
Felix: Good Fairy Dewdrop, can you not give a practical hint to aid us in our quest?
Dewdrop: (*selfrighteously*) You have undertaken the task and therefore you must help yourself. But I will give you one clue; there are several keys to Harmony. Once you have found these, you will be able to unlock the door to the kingdom. Good luck go with you. Farewell! (*Picks up bag and goes out right to the strains of 'harp music'*).

Sound Effects Cue 10
Felix: She's a dead loss! And we could have well done without the sermon. Do you know I think I prefer Discord. At least he has some character.
Augustus: Master Felix, do not be a traitor to your own cause.
Hilarius: Do not be so hard on poor Dewdrop. She is a brilliant student and gained a double first in thaumaturgy (*a meaningful glance at Augustus*)—magic, you know.
Augustus: (*haughtily*) I do know.
Hilarius: She is still growing up and the young are notoriously inarticulate though vociferous concerning their ideals. But one day she will be a conventional fairy, dispensing lightness and sweet . . . .
Augustus: Sweetness and light.

ACT ONE THE HAPPY WIZARD

Felix: A sickly mixture! Nevertheless she was right about self help. And we must not forget that vital clue about the keys. Don't let's waste any more time. Come, we must go.

Penny: (*wearily*) If we be going to walk, I can't. My poor feet be killing me.

Augustus: (*bowing mockingly*) Then madam will perforce have to ride on Shank's pony.

Felix: That gives me an idea. Hilarius, can't you conjure up some horses?

Hilarius: I don't see why not. Just a moment while I rub off some of the rust. (*Rubs wand*) That's better. Now where did I put my recipe book of spells? (*Searches pockets and takes out note book*) The instructions are somewhere in the middle: (*leafs through book*) Hamsters, handkerchiefs coloured, handkerchiefs plain, hats, hedgehogs . . . . . . hurricanes. Oh dear! The horse page is missing.

Augustus: Look under mounts, chargers, steeds . . . . . .

Felix: Or even under mules and donkeys.

Hilarius: (*sadly*) It's no use, they were all on the same page.

Felix: Try to remember the spell. Concentrate.

Hilarius: I'll try. (*Chants*)
 Abra cadabra, riddle me ree,
 Please send horses, one, two, three . . . .

Sound Effects Cue 11

(*There is a whinney off stage left*).

Penny: (*gleefully*) It's worked, it's worked. Methinks I heard a whinney in yonder spinney. (*Points left*).

Felix: You may be right Miss Penelope. Now Augustus, will you be so good as to go and collect our mounts. (*Augustus goes off left and returns immediately, struggling with a wooden clothes horse*).

Felix: (*ruefully*) Hilarius, my friend, I think you've backed the wrong horse. Never mind, we'll just have to go on foot.

Music Cue 5

(*They go out right, skipping in time to the music and singing more verses of Back in the Book as the curtain falls*).

All: Back in the book,
That's where we'll look,
We must find the kingdom by hook or by crook.
Back to the text.
Whatever next
Will plague us and tease us and leave us perplexed?
Tra la la la la lah, etc.

Lighting Cue 14

BLACKOUT

ACT 1
Scene 2

Music Cue 6

The village green at Little Woody Bottom. Penny's pretty thatched cottage with its hanging sign bearing the legend 'Heavenshire Dream Teas' is upstage right, and various small tables and chairs are scattered in front of the house. A large cut out of a chestnut tree in full bloom is upstage left. Under this is a rustic bench. The sun is shining.

Lighting Cue 15

Billy Pippin, a yokel whose face resembles a rosy wrinkled apple is lying on the bench, snoring gently. He wears a holland smock and battered hat. Daffy-down-Dilly, a pretty but not so simple village maiden, enters right. She goes up to Billy and shakes his shoulder.

Daffy: Billy!
Billy: (*sleepily*) Ay?
Daffy: Are you asleep again?
Billy: Ar!
Daffy: Then you just start sleep walking and help me arrange these tables before the customers come.
Billy: Oh! Ah! (*Yawns and goes to sleep again*)
(*Sally enters from the cottage, carrying table cloths and cutlery. Despite her simple dress she looks every inch a fairy tale heroine*).
Sally: Hallo, Daffy! Isn't it a glorious afternoon?
Daffy: 'Afternoon, Miss Sally. But what's glorious about it? It's Monday.
Sally: And what's wrong with Monday?
Daffy: Work. (*She helps Sally set the tables*).
Sally: Never mind. You'll be off duty by six o'clock. By the way, did you happen to meet Aunt Penny as you came through the village?
She went out quite early this morning and hasn't come back.

THE HAPPY WIZARD   ACT ONE

Daffy: Don't worry Miss Sally. She's probably gone to the new supermarket in Great Woody Bottom. I do hope she brings the grocery back with her, otherwise I don't know what we are going to give the customers for tea.

Sally: If there are any customers. Unless things improve we shall have to close the tea garden.

Daffy: It won't come to that, Miss. You know, miss, I don't like to see a girl like you slaving away here all day when you ought to be out enjoying yourself. I wish you could meet a nice young man and get married.

Sally: And spend my time slaving away for him? No, thank you! In any case there aren't any young men for me to marry. Billy Pippin's the only bachelor left in the village and somehow I don't think we would suit one another.

Daffy: *(firmly)* Billy Pippin's my intended We are being married next month.

Sally: But how exciting! I am so glad for you Daffy. I must wake up your lazy good for nothing fiancé and give him my congratulations.

Daffy: *(catching her by the arm)* No, Miss Sally! Don't do that because he doesn't know anything about it yet. I intend it to be a surprise so that he won't have time to change his mind. *(Blissfully)* It's such a wonderful feeling, knowing your future is assured.

Sally: *(in a wry voice)* It must be.

Daffy: I do wish you could find someone like my Billy.

Sally: What would be the point? I must devote my life to taking care of Aunt Penny. I can never repay her kindness.

Daffy: Do you remember the time when you were a little girl and your father was the head chef at the Royal Palace in Mythuania? Things were so different then.

Sally: *(sitting at one of the tables)* Indeed they were. We had our own quarters in the east wing of the palace. And the Queen used to give parties for the children of all the palace employees; the late King insisted that his son attended those parties, because he thought it a good idea for the Prince to mix with his subjects; but Felix was a horrid conceited boy who used to tease all the girls. And I don't suppose he has changed very much.

Daffy: I've heard he has grown into a very handsome young man and now that he is king he will have to marry sooner or later. Wouldn't it be romantic if you and he could meet again and fall in love and . . . .

Sally: That's enough of this foolish talk. Such a ridiculous situation could not possibly arise: and even if it did I wouldn't marry that stuck up young man if he were the last man left in this earth. Please get on with your work.

Daffy: (*mutters*) Famous last words.

Sally: Now Daffy, we musn't waste any more time. Will you go into the kitchen and put the kettle on please. If I know Aunt Penny the first thing she will want when she comes home is a nice cup of tea.

Daffy: Yes, miss. (*She goes into cottage. Sally puts a few finishing touches to the tables then sits down on one of the stools*).

Music Cue 7

Sally: Dear Aunt Penny, I owe so much to her that I could never consider leaving her. But had things been different, I wonder if I should have fallen in love? (*Sings*)

Music Cue 8

DREAMING DREAMS

Just dreaming dreams,
Taking flights of fancy
From Jupiter to Mars,
Romantic schemes,
Building Spanish castles
Way up among the stars.
All my life's been spent in chasing rainbows,
Looking for the sunshine when the rain goes.
But now it seems
All my schemes must vanish
Like smoke rings in the blue,
And all my dreams
Will fade because there's no
One to make them come true.

Now Sally Lunn, stop all this self indulgence and get on with some work. (*Starts to busy herself with the tables as Daffy rushes out of the cottage*).

Daffy: I've just looked out of the kitchen window and seen your Auntie coming down the lane—with three strange gentlemen.
Sally: Who can they be? Oh, probably just customers. Have we got enough scones?
Daffy: Yes, I think so. But you ought to see them. The gentlemen, I mean. There's a young handsome one, magnificently dressed: a middle aged one who looks a bit like a schoolmaster and a tall elderly one in a sort of wizard's hat. I wonder if they could be strolling players?

Music Cue 9

Sally: Possibly, but we shan't make much profit if they are. We must go into the kitchen and start buttering scones. (*They go into the cottage as Penny with Hilarius, Felix and Augustus enter from the left. They look very weary and worn as they make a brave effort to sing more verses of 'Back in the Book'*).

Music Cue 10

All: Back in the book,
Searched ev'ry nook,
Can't find the kingdom wherever we look.
What a to-do,
What can we do
To dispel the spell of Discord's ballyhoo?
Tra la etc.
Penny: This is my hive,
Here's where I thrive,
Just as I told you we've reached chapter five.
Hilarius: Oh my poor feet!
Find me a seat,
I've walked all the way in the dust and the heat.
Tra la etc.
Felix: Oh what a pace,
It's been a race,
Here we can rest from our quest for a space.
Hilarius: This will suit me,
Hope you agree,
Here's the tea garden I vote we have tea.
All: Tra la etc.

ACT ONE THE HAPPY WIZARD

Augustus: I don't agree,
For don't you see,
We haven't had lunch so how can we have tea?
Hilarius: Fiddle dee dee,
Sit down prithee,
My ankles are worn down right up to the knee.
All: Tra la etc.
Felix: Gentlemen please,
Pray take your ease,
I'll order refreshment your thirst to appease.
Penny: Please take a chair,
I will repair
Now unto my lair some good fare to prepare.
All: Tra la etc.
Penny: I'll send one of my handmaidens to wait upon you. Daffy!
(The three men subside onto stools).
Daffy: *(rushing out of cottage)* Thank goodness you are back safely. Miss Sally was getting worried about you.
Penny: There was no need to be worried. I have been in very good company. Now gentlemen, if you will excuse me I be going to superintend the preparations for your lunch. Take the order, Daffy. *(With a gay little wave she disappears into the house).*
Daffy: But we don't do lunches! Oh well, I suppose I'd better do as I am told. *(Takes out notebook and pencil from apron pocket)* What will it be, kind sirs?
Felix: My secretary will order.
Augustus: We will commence with turtle soup, then sole veronique, saddle of lamb, new potatoes and petits pois, peaches in brandy with clotted cream, followed by angels on horseback and a selection of cheeses. Coffee and liqueurs to conclude our meal, of course. May I see your wine list?
Daffy: *(she has been listening open mouthed)* Oh dear, we haven't got anything like that. I didn't know lambs wore saddles, but perhaps we could cut off a bit of old Dobbin's harness, if that would do. As for our cheese, well, we'd had it a long time you see, and it walked out last Friday, although it was chained up in the larder.
Augustus: Then what have you got on today?

Daffy:	Well—there's my clean apron, yellow dress, a green petticoat, an orange petticoat, a white petticoat . . . .
Augustus:	(*horrified*) Enough!
Daffy:	No, sir! There's a cool breeze today.
Augustus:	In words of one syllable—what can we have to eat?
Daffy:	I'd better go and ask in the kitchen. (*Exits at the same time calling out*) Billy! Wake up. You'll have to come and help me. (*Billy gets up and shambles after her*).
Felix:	Do use your imagination, Augustus, this is only a rustic café, not the royal banqueting hall.
Augustus:	I was only trying to please your majesty by ordering the favourite royal dishes.
Felix:	I understood we had agreed to travel as private citizens. Please bear that in mind for we are now in Pantomania, and as you are well aware my country has no official diplomatic relations with the Pantomaniacs.
Hilarius:	I am only an old nit-wit, no, wit-nit of a wizard and thus do not understand your international affairs. Please put me in the portrait.
Felix:	Picture. This trouble started many years ago when I was a small boy and my mother was Queen Regent. As you may have gathered from Augustus she is a woman of determination and fixed ideas.
Augustus:	Pray do not criticise your royal mother. (*bows*) Queen Tryphena (*bows*) is a truly great woman of immense depth of character . . . .
Felix:	(*interrupting*) And you, my friend, are terrified of her! But I was not being unkind about my mother, merely stating a fact. Now as I was saying, Pantomania was then a province of Mythuania under the authority of a local council responsible to the Queen Regent. But the Pantomaniacs wanted total independence and my mother considered the time was not ripe. As you can now see they are a simple and unsophisticated people.
Augustus:	After many months of trying negotiations a special messenger called on the Queen (*bows*) and handed her a parchment. It contained a unilateral declaration of independence, and since that awful day Queen Tryphena (*bows*) will not have the matter mentioned in her presence.

ACT ONE THE HAPPY WIZARD

Hilarius: But now that you are king cannot you do anything to restore good relations?
Felix: What is the point? The Mythuanian Empire was given away years ago and we have no longer any right to call ourselves a colonial power. Since U.D.I. the Pantomaniacs have done very well for themselves despite sanctions. Their agriculture is booming. *(Points)* Look through that gap in the trees at those acres of ripe waving corn which they harvest every Christmas. The custard pie industry is booming and in the field of literature their authors lead the world in shaggy dog stories. The Pantomaniacs are doing even better than the mother country.
Hilarius: A pity that there should be this estrangement.
(Daffy re-enters and curtsies to the three).
Daffy: Would you care for a saucepan of soup, Sirs?
Augustus: *(hautily)* Gentlemen, I assume that this person, this menial, this hireling, abigail, skivvy is indicating that a soupçon of soup is available.
(Daffy looks indignant).
Felix: Do not mind my learned friend. He does not mean to be rude but long ago he swallowed a dictionary and regurgitates words like the wind.
Daffy: Very good, sir. I'll bring the bicarbonate along with the soup. *(Goes to cottage)* Billy! Is the soup ready?
Billy: *(off stage)* Ar.
Daffy: Then hand me the tray through the window.
Billy: Ay. *(He does so and she brings a tray of three steaming bowls to the customers' table).*
Daffy: Your soup, gentlemen.
Hilarius: And I am ready for it. My rummy is beginning to tumble.
(They begin to drink the soup).
Felix: *(collecting something on the end of his spoon)* What in the world can this be?
Augustus: *(peering at the object in the dish)* It appears uncommonly like that delicacy known to the lower classes as tripe.
Daffy: *(in horror)* Oh sir! Let me take the soup away. I think that's the knitted dishcloth I lost this morning. I'll get you something else. *(Puts soup bowls on tray).*
Augustus: Bring me a little fish—and I do not mean a minnow
Daffy: The fish is off, sir.

34

THE HAPPY WIZARD ACT ONE

Hilarius: Then I take it we have also had our chips?
Daffy: No, sir. We don't serve chips.
Felix: Then some nice tender cutlets?
Daffy: Sorry. They're off.
Felix: Then what can we have?
Daffy: Meat Pie?
Felix: Very well.
Daffy: But I shouldn't have it if I were you.
Felix: (*exasperated*) Why not?
Daffy: It's off.
Felix: But you said it was on.
Daffy: It is, but it's going off—it's last week's.
Hilarius: I'd like a nice toad in the hole.
Daffy: Sorry, we haven't got no holes.
Augustus: Then we had better settle for three cups of coffee.
Daffy: No coffee, only tea, sir. Billy!
Billy: (*through window*) Ay?
Daffy: I've got three awkward customers here. They can't make up their minds what they want.
Billy: Oh!
Daffy: Better get me three mugs of cocoa.
Billy: Oh, ar. Three mugs coming up. (*He hands them through the window*).
Daffy: (*bringing them over to table*) Here you are, sirs.
Felix: What is this witch's brew?
Daffy: No, Billy's. I think it might be some home made wine. I know what you would like I'll see if Billy can do you a special. Billy!
Billy: Ay?
Daffy: Has the cat come back?
Billy: Ar.
Daffy: Did she bring anything in with her?
Billy: Ar.
Daffy: Then take it off her and serve up the speciality of the house.
Billy: Ar. (*Withdraws from the window*).
Augustus: I do not like this hostelry. The atmosphere is suspicious and I smell a rodent.
Daffy: (*surprised*) How did you guess, sir?
Felix: This is too much. The bill if you please.
Daffy: (*as she goes into the house*) Billy, you're wanted.

Sound Effects Cue 12
(*a fanfare is heard in the distance*).

ACT ONE THE HAPPY WIZARD

Hilarius: Listen! (*Fanfare again, nearer*).
Sound Effects Cue 13
Felix: (*going left and peering offstage*) It's a herald, wearing the insignia of our royal household. He's coming this way and we are bound to be recognised. Let us hide. (*The three crowd behind the chestnut tree*). Be quiet and listen carefully.
(*There is a flash and Discord enters left wearing a richly embroidered tabard and plumed hat. He carries a trumpet attached to which is a banner embellished with the arms of Mythuania. He is followed by a crowd of villagers. Penny, Daffy, Sally and Billy come out of the house to listen*).
Discord: Oyez, oyez, oyez.
Hear ye all ye citizens of Pantomania,
This proclamation of Her Imperial Majesty
The Dowager Queen Tryphena of Mythuania.
It is with great distress
No words can 'ere express
That we announce our son
The youthful king is gone.
He's missing from the palace
And enemies with malice
May have him in captivity.
Or maybe in disguise he goes
He's often done so, goodness knows.
And though we place no veto
On his wandering incognito,
Yet it's surely fraught with danger
For he really is no stranger
To the enemies we've mentioned.
Hear ye then for gold we offer
From our almost empty coffer
A reward—five hundred pounds
For the one by whom he's found.
And since King Felix has no bride,
Ladies, seek him far and wide!
And if maiden pure and simple
Free from blemish, spot and pimple
Finds our king and breaks this deadlock
She shall have his hand in wedlock!
Here endeth the proclamation.
Oyez, oyez, oyez.

Lighting Cue 16

Sound Effects Cue 14

(*there is a flash and a clap of thunder and Discord goes out left. The villagers disperse excitedly. Daffy, Sally, Penny and Billy go back into the house. As the noise dies away the three fugitives emerge from behind the tree*).

Felix: We must leave here immediately. It was obvious my mother would take extreme measures once the postman delivered the crown, but I never imagined she would go so far as to marry me off to the damsel who discovered my whereabouts. This girl might be anyone, a serving wench or a gipsy. Wait a moment now, there's something peculiar about all this. My mother is a stickler for protocol and she would never countenance my marrying a commoner. Therefore the latter part of the proclamation does not ring true.

Hilarius: The herald's voice reminded me of Discord—maybe he waylaid the real messenger, stole his clothes and altered the proclamation to suit his own ends. I told you he was a master of disguise.

Augustus: May I venture my humble opinion? (*Felix nods*). I think that Discord, with his silver tongue may have persuaded Her Majesty (*bows*) that by taking this course she might yet realise a great ambition, namely the reunion of Pantomania with Mythuania . . . .

Felix: I see what you mean—if a Pantomanian girl claims the reward the ensuing marriage would automatically bring about a permanent political alliance. This makes it all important that we escape from Pantomania. So far we have been lucky and have not been recognised, but with such a reward in the offing the whole female population will be on the look out for us: and if Penny Bunn or whatever the old duck's name is puts two and two together, we are lost.

Hilarius: Your Majesty, I mean Felix, do you think you should continue to help me? In the circumstances I shall understand if you decide to give up and return to your own country.

ACT ONE THE HAPPY WIZARD

Felix: No, Hilarius, I intend to keep my promise. No doubt my mother will eventually get her wish and marry me off to some stuffy girl, but I'm determined to make the most of my freedom for the time being. Why, my own imperial guard may be out hunting for me—what a dance I will lead them.

Hilarius: Many, many thanks. You have proved such a good friend to a poor tizzy old dizzard in a wizzy.

Augustus: (*slowly*) A dizzy old wizard in a tizzy.

Felix: Do make allowances for Augustus—he can never forget he was once a tutor and teachers always lecture, never converse. Now let's get down to making some plans. If we are to evade capture . . . . .

Augustus: (*sinks onto a stool in despair*) Capture! If we are caught I shall never be able to convince Her Majesty (*bows*) that it was not I who lead you astray. I shall be flung into a dungeon, for life.

Felix: (*pats him on shoulder*) Do not worry, old friend, it may never happen.

Hilarius: And a sentence in a modern prison is rather like a session in a holiday camp, so I have heard.

Augustus That is what frightens me.

Felix: (*looking up and pointing*) A pigeon! He's circling round and round.

Hilarius: Have a care Master Felix, such a bird may be in the employ of Discord and you are a marked man.

Felix: Not yet.

(*Three pairs of eyes follow the flight of the unseen bird. Something drops from the flies*).

Hilarius: Everybody duck! (*They do so. Then Felix picks up the fallen object*).

Felix: Good heavens! Two silver keys.

Hilarius: Let me see. There's an inscription on one of them. It reads 'This is the key of friendship which will open one of the doors to Harmony'. Why, it's my own front door key. Goody goody drop gums, no gum drops! The other one is the key of Trust and looks remarkably like the one to my back porch.

Augustus Now all that remains is to find the doors.

Felix: These are the first clues, but we haven't exactly found them, they seem to have found us. What have we done to deserve this bit of luck?

Hilarius: Perhaps you have earned them by giving me your promise of friendship and loyalty.

Felix:	Maybe. That would bear out Dewdrop-the-do-gooder's little homily. I hope the rest of the clues are not so obscure. But we must not delay. I don't altogether trust that serving maid or her mistress, but we must not depart without settling the account.
Augustus	(*calls*) Varlet! Hither!
	(*Billy looks through window*)
Billy:	Ay?
Augustus	Tell your mistress we would have speech with her.
Billy:	Oh ar! (*Disappears from window*).
Felix:	It may be necessary for us to separate at times so we must set up headquarters where we can meet or leave messages.
	(*Billy appears at window and listens*).
Hilarius:	Then we must cross the frontier into the Land of Legend. Near the border there is an old ruin of a windmill which would make a very good hiding place.
Felix:	Excellent. You must be our guide.
	(*Sally appears and Billy ducks out of sight*).
Felix:	I was under the impression that we sent for Miss Penelope Bunn.
Sally:	I am Sally Lunn, Miss Bunn's niece. My Aunt is very weary and trying to get some rest. May I be of any help?
Augustus	(*disdainfully*) We wish to settle the account. But I must make it known that neither my companions nor myself have ever before encountered such disgraceful service as in this so called restaurant. The food is disgusting, the staff impertinent and the entire establishment is suspect. Have you anything to say?
Sally:	Yes, I have. Your attitude is unreasonable. We are ordinary villagers and unused to fine society as you so obviously are. We live simply and cater for the needs of simple people. How could you expect to be served with a banquet in a rustic tea garden? As for payment, I will not accept a penny! (*Turns away*).
Felix:	Throw her a bag of gold. She will soon change her tune when she hears the chink of coins.
	(*Augustus does so. Sally fields it neatly and throws it back*).
Sally:	Don't be insulting. Please leave immediately. Penelope Bunn and Sally Lunn may be poor and homely but at least they are well bred.

Felix: Half baked, in my opinion.
Sally: I would sooner be half baked than hard boiled. Good day! (*She flounces into the cottage*).
Hilarius: Good master Felix, you were a little hard on our bucolic beauty. Sally Lunn is a very tasty little tea cake, do you not agree? If I were a mortal and thirty years younger that tasty little tea cake would be just my cup of tea.
Felix: I suppose she has plenty of spirit and no one can deny she is beautiful, but that does not excuse her treatment of persons of the blood royal.
Hilarius: But she does not know your real identity.
Felix: I had forgotten that. Maybe I should have tempered my behaviour, but it is too late now, and I am afraid I have to admit it is not possible for me to eat humble pie.
Hilarius: My dear boy, you have much to learn. The divine right of kings does not exist outside your fictitious little kingdom.
Augustus Are you informing His Maj . . . . Master Felix that he cannot expect obedience and respect outside Mythuania?
Hilarius: Obedience, no, and respect only if he earns it. But, if I may make so bold as to say so, as a fugitive he must not attract undue attention by arrogant behaviour.
Felix: Point taken. But as I am unlikely to encounter this maiden again I shall have no opportunity to apologise. Come, gentlemen, we must away. I will take the field path; you, Augustus, keep to the highway, but stay close to the hedges. Hilarius, remain here for about ten minutes and then follow in my track. I will wait for you by the first blasted oak. We will rendezvous with Augustus at the old mill at sunset.
(*Felix and Augustus go out leaving Hilarius sitting at one of the tables. Suddenly he sees Felix's cloak which has been left behind*).
Hilarius: Oh bother! The king has forgotten his cloak. He'll never learn. Never mind, I will take it with me when I follow him.

Sound Effects Cue 15
(*Sound of harp music and Dewdrop appears right. Hilarius drops cloak*).
Hello! It's my friend Drop in. How nice of you to Dewdrop on your rounds.

Dewdrop: (*in best District Nurse manner*) And how are we progressing this afternoon?

Hilarius: A little better, I think. Felix now has two of the keys, a very good sign. I wish there was something positive I could do to help, but these days I am such a middle headed old wuzard, such a widdle headed old muddard . . . .

Dewdrop: Hm. You do go from bad to worse. But never mind. I have been studying Felix's case and have decided on a specific type of treatment. I need your co-operation. (*Hilarius nods eagerly*) We must find a way of safeguarding Felix just in case he does not find Harmony within the given time. Neither of us would wish to see him married to Penelope, but Sally is a very different proposition. Now just supposing he were to be married to Sally before the end of the week . . . . . .

Hilarius: Then he couldn't marry Penelope! (*Then sadly shakes his head*) But it won't do, it won't do. They don't like one another. A pity.

Dewdrop: Hilarius, if you were a woman you would know that when two people of the opposite sex start by hating one another they invariably finish up in each other's arms.

Hilarius: How can you be so sure that they are suited?

Dewdrop: I fed their statistics and characteristics into the Cupid Computer. The cards came out as perfect affinities.

Hilarius: I know I'm only an old duddy fuddy, but this method seems to be a very cold blooded way of matchmaking.

Dewdrop: Not at all. We must make good use of modern science and technology. I concentrated on this during my last term at college. Now before I go to set up operation love match I had better check my equipment. (*Opens black bag and takes out aerosol*).

Hilarius: What's that?

Dewdrop: Romantic atmosphere to be sprayed around the old mill. Smell. (*Sprays*).

ACT ONE THE HAPPY WIZARD

Hilarius: (*sniffs*). It's rather like some kind of anaesthetic.
Dewdrop: Exactly. It makes the process of falling in love less painful. (*Searches in bag and takes out cassette*). Recorded song of nightingales just in case the real birds are on strike. It has a soothing effect. (*Takes out gun*).
Hilarius: (*retreats in alarm*). What's that frightening piece of apparatus?
Dewdrop: A gun. It fires heart penetrating darts tipped with serum taken from the love bug. It enters the blood stream immediately with instantaneous results. Much more accurate than Cupid's old fashioned bow and arrows.
Hilarius: That worked very well in the olden days.
Dewdrop: Come now, we must move with the times. Fairy knows best. Where's the spray of silicone polish? Must give the moon an instant shine. Oh there it is. (*Repacks bag*).
Now for your part in this little plot. I want you to try and bring Felix and Sally together on every possible occasion. I do believe he left his cloak here?
Hilarius: Yes, there it is.
Dewdrop: Then leave it. Sally will find it.
Hilarius: But she won't know what to do with it.
Dewdrop: Not to worry. All that is in hand. It will go just according to plan, you'll see. (*Collects bag*) I'm going now. Must be in good time to set the tender trap at the old mill. Farewell! (*Goes out right*).
Hilarius: Welfare! I mean farewell! I suppose Dewdrop knows what she is doing, she seems to have become frightfully efficient so I'll do exactly as she says. But wait a moment. She has given me an idea for another plan, one that will make doubly sure that Felix cannot be forced to marry Penny Bunn. I'll marry her off to Augustus. She will be far from unwilling. but he will hate it. Augustus is a very clever man but he has been unnecessarily uppity with me on occasions and he needs to be taught a lesson. What an arch bride for an archduke! (*Chuckles*) I'm too ancient to use Dewdrop's methods but the good old love potion usually works. Now what shall I start with? (*Looks around and sees bottle on table*) Ah! Elderberry wine, the very thing. Now what can I put in it to make it really potent? A few herbs, I think.

THE HAPPY WIZARD   ACT ONE

(*Flits about taking leaves and flowers from the bushes round the green*).
There's rosemary for remembrance, violets for modesty, hm, better leave those out. Moonbeams for illusion, oh dear, it's still daylight. Well, perhaps a sunbeam will do, it might just have a slight dazzling effect; orange blossom for wedding bells. Now what else? Oh, I know! A spoonful of sugar for sweetness, a pinch of salt to bring out the flavour and a touch of the hot stuff—mustard! Shake it up well. Now to write the directions on the bottle. (*Takes quill pen from inside hat*).

Music Cue 11

To be taken three times a day, before, during and after meals. That should do the trick. I'll leave it where Miss Penelope will be sure to find it. This should cause quite a bit of fun. (*Song and dance clutching bottle*).

Music Cue 12

THE MIXTURE

I've a naughty little notion,
To distil a magic potion,
And create an ocean of devotion
In the heart of Penny Bunn.

I've a certain little notion,
That a little dose of lotion,
Will incite emotion and commotion
In the hearts of all and one.

Hocus pocus, mumbo jumbo,
Helter skelter, broomstick, mumbo,
Bell and candle, book and almanac!
Fiddle diddle, fylfot, fizzle,
Hoo doo, voo doo, philtre, swizzle,
Spell and cantrip, aphrodisiac!

So I'll set my plan in motion,
And concoct my magic potion,
And 'tis my unshakeable prenotion
That's it's going to be fun!

(*Hilarius finishes his little dance and sinks breathlessly into a chair, dumping the bottle on the table. Daffy enters from cottage*).

ACT ONE　　　　THE HAPPY WIZARD

Daffy: Sir, you must not do things like that here. Miss Penny isn't licensed for singing and dancing. Here's a new penny to go away and sing somewhere else.

Hilarius: So sorry, Miss Dilly down Daffy. But you keep it, your need may be greater than mine. (*Goes out humming happily and forgetting to pick up his wand*).

Lighting Cue 17

Daffy: Dotty old man! Thank goodness he's gone. (*Calls*) Miss Sally! Shall I clear away?

Sally: (*emerging from cottage*) Yes, Daffy. I'm coming to help you. I don't think there will be any more customers today. Business seems to be getting worse.

Daffy: I know miss, and we've had so many complaints.

Sally: (*collecting plates, etc.*) Don't let it upset you. Fortunately there aren't many people as rude as the three who came this afternoon. Even though trade is bad we can do without that type of customer.

Daffy: I know. Still, what can you expect? They were men!

Sally: That's an unusual remark for you to make. I thought you were fond of the opposite sex.

Daffy: I am, but I pretend I'm not. (*Confidentially*) It sort of spurs them on.

Sally: I see, or at least I think I do. But isn't it likely to lead to complications? What if you *don't* like any particular one?

Daffy: I like them all!

Sally: Daffy, you are incorrigible. Oh bother! That awful young man has left his cloak. (*Picks it up and examines it*) It's rather gorgeous, isn't it? The material is beautiful and of such good quality. Daffy, look at this gold thread embroidery—these motifs. What do they look like to you?

Daffy: A sort of letter F?

Sally: I think so too. This cloak is obviously expensive and it is very careless of that young man to leave it lying around. But I suppose rich people can afford to be careless. He may come back for it so I'll put it away safely in the house.

Daffy:	He won't come back. If you ask me those three are up to no good. They are desperate criminals. You heard that proclamation, didn't you? I think they may have murdered the king and stolen his cloak and bag of gold. You mark my words. My Billy heard them talking and making plans to separate and meet up at the old mill in the Land of Legend. Rich young men don't do things like that. That place has a bad reputation and if you ask me there's something very fishy going on.
Sally:	I didn't ask you and you are letting your imagination run away with you. They don't look like murderers. I'll take this cloak to the mill and hand it back.
Daffy:	Don't you go miss. Send Billy with it.
Sally:	(*folding cloak*). No. Something tells me I must go myself. If I hurry I can be there and back by sundown. And if we were to keep the cloak here that odious young man might return and accuse us of stealing it. Tell Aunt Penny I won't be long. (*Goes out*).
Daffy:	Don't say I didn't warn you. (*Collects up more cutlery*). If Miss Sally wakes up tomorrow morning strangulated and with her throat cut from ear to ear I shall tell her I told her so!
	(*Penny comes out of cottage*).
Penny:	Have the gentlemen gone already?
Daffy:	Ages ago and jolly good riddance.
Penny:	Don't be rude, Daffy. How many times be I telling you not to let your tongue run away with you? (*sinks down into chair*) I don't expect we'll be seeing them again and this is the end of an exciting epsiode in my life. When a body reaches the age of forty-five, well fifty, her chances of meeting a suitable suitor be less and less. (*Wistfully*) I did like the clever one who spoke all those long words. I couldn't understand all he said but it did sound so lovely. (*To Daffy*) I haven't had the schooling you young ones have had.
Daffy:	Don't ever trust a gentleman who talks too much, Miss Penny. (*Picks up wand*) Good gracious! What's this funny little stick with a rusty star on the end of it?
Penny:	It's the wizard's magic wand. What a wonderful stroke of luck! Let me have it and I will wave it and make a wish.

Daffy: (*reluctantly handing it over*) Best leave well alone. It doesn't pay mortals to meddle with magic.
Penny: Do you really think so? But nothing will go wrong. Now shall I wish to be young and beautiful?
Daffy: I shouldn't. Remember what happened to Mother Goose; she was only too glad to be old and ugly again.
Penny: Then I'll have a night out like Cinderella. I wish to go to a ball in a silver dress, escorted by Mr. Augustus in a coach drawn by six white horses.

Sound Effects Cue 16

(*Waves wand but no coach appears, only Nelly the Nightmare, a perfect disaster of a pantomime type horse. She whinnies and capers gracefully round the village green*).

Lighting Cue 18

Penny: (*sadly*). No coach, no Augustus, no silver dress. (*Cheers up*) But a dear little horse. What's your name dear? Let me look on your collar. It says 'I am Nelly the Nightmare—if lost return to finder'. But I'm the finder. That means she's mine.
Daffy: I don't think you should keep her. If the wizard finds out he will be frightfully annoyed. Wave the wand and send her back.
Penny: (*stroking Nelly*) I have a better plan. She be the wizard's horse that's for sure. Horses are clever and I've heard stories about lost horses who found their way back to their masters. I'll go with Nelly and let her have her head. We'll take the wand and give it back to Hilarius. And Daffy, I might even meet Mr. Augustus again. You do know the way, don't you Nelly? (*Nelly nods*). There Daffy, I told you so.
Daffy: Your fine gentlemen all went off to the old mill, my Billy told me, and Miss Sally's gone after them with the young one's cloak.
Penny: Sally's gone to that lonely place? That settles it. It's not right for a young girl to be out alone after sundown. I must go and bring her back. Billy!
Billy: Ah!

Penny: (*he looks through window*) Bring me out a basket of provisions. It's quite a long journey and Sally and I may have to stop for our supper on the way back.
(*Billy enters with a basket*) Put in that bottle of elderberry wine. (*Billy takes bottle from table*).

Music Cue 13

Now then Nelly dear let us be getting acquainted.
(*Penny leads Nelly as she sings*)

Music Cue 14

GIDDY-YUP, NELLY

Giddy-yup Nelly,
Take me for a ride,
Clip clop merrily
Through the countryside.

Cantering gaily
Saddle on the side,
For no fine lady
Ever rides astride.

So proudly mounted
In the manner born,
Just like a damsel
Riding with the Quorn.

Clearing the hedges
High up in the air,
Taking the fences
With a foot to spare.

Out with the Belvoir,
Raise the stirrup cup,
Come home wearily
When the hunt is up.

Come along Nelly,
Tighten up your girth,
Must find Augustus
'ere he goes to earth!

Come along Billy, help me mount. Hand me up my basket, Daffy. *(Somehow they manage to heave Penny onto Nelly's back).* Tally Ho! We're off! *(She is, and Nelly gallops off followed by Penny desperately clinging to the nightmare's tail).*

Lighting Cue 19

Lighting Cue 20

BLACKOUT.

Lighting Cue 21
Music Cue 15 (Entracte)
Lighting Cue 22

ACT II

Lighting Cue 23 and 24

> The picturesque ruin of the old mill is in the shape of a cut-out silhouetted against the night sky. There is a practical door in the mill. At the back of the stage is a groundrow showing a range of hills, with a castle on top of one of these. There is a clump of trees (cut outs) upstage right downstage of which is a grassy bank, on which Felix is found seated. An owl hoots once or twice. The scene is both eerie and beautiful. Unseen by Felix, Dewdrop enters up stage right and flits about with her aerosol. Having sprayed to her satisfaction she takes cover behind a tree.

Music Cue 16 (Softly)
Sound Effects Cue 17

Felix: (*to himself*) It is almost moonrise and Augustus should have been here hours ago. I suppose I should go and look for him, but if I do I may miss Hilarius and we shall all be wandering round in circles looking for one another. Oh! Someone's coming. I'd better take cover in case it's an enemy. (*Withdraws into shadow of trees as Hilarius enters humming a snatch of song*). Oh, it's you Hilarius. (*Emerges from trees*) Don't make so much noise. Remember we are fugitives and you are making a din loud enough to wake the dead.

Hilarius: I know. But I'm full of the joys of living. It's a wonderful feeling, don't you know?

Felix: Are you about to tell me you've found your kingdom by yourself and all our troubles are over?

Hilarius: No. But before long our luck will change—you'll see.

Felix: It is to be hoped you are right. Have you seen Augustus? He is so late I am beginning to fear some misfortune may have befallen him.

ACT TWO　　　　　THE HAPPY WIZARD

Hilarius: Dear, dear! (*Aside*) If something has happened to the wretched little man my little plan will be no good. (*To Felix*) You don't think he has been attacked by vogues and ragabonds?

Felix: More likely to have been taken prisoner by a contingent of my Royal Mythuanian guard, in which case I shall have to post straight back to the palace in order to bail him out of the deepest dungeon into which my royal Mama will have had him thrown. But this is looking on the black side—he's probably waiting for moonrise to enable him to find his way here. Nevertheless I have an uneasy feeling in my bones.

Hilarius: In the meantime, Master Felix, just relax and enjoy this perfect summer evening. Breathe in the soft air of the Land of Legend, gaze upon the stars twinkling in the night sky, listen to . . . .

Felix: Stop!

Lighting Cue 25

Hilarius: (*to himself*) Steady, Hilarius, mustn't overdo it now. (*To Felix*) But can't you scent something; something unusual in the air? (*Sniffs loudly*).

Felix: Not really, unless it's the smell from the moat round the old castle over there.

Hilarius: (*turning away sadly*) So much for Dewdrop's aerosol. (*Tries again*) But didn't you hear the nightingales when you came through the woods?

Felix: All I've heard for the last hour or so are two owls in a tree over there. I've watched their yellow eyes staring at me; it was most disconcerting. Are they birds of ill omen?

Hilarius: Gracious goodness, no. That wise old bird brought his lady friend here with but one thing in mind—to wit, to woo.

Felix: Or to hunt for mice in the moonlight! Quiet! I can hear footsteps. (*Pulls Hilarius into shadows*) It's that silly serving wench and the scoundrelly scullion. I thought we had left all those Pantomaniacs way behind us in Little Woody Bottom. Obviously they heard the proclamation, put two and two together and followed us here, hot on our trail.

Hilarius: I don't think there is any need to worry about those two. They have only come to this secluded spot to do

	a little courting. What it is to be young my boy! Just listen to all that billing and cooing. Take note of it —you may well pick up a few useful hints.
Felix:	I think not.

Lighting Cue 26

	(*Billy and Daffy enter up right, holding hands*).
Daffy:	(*softly*) Bill!
Billy:	(*coyly*) Coo!
Daffy:	(*a little louder*) Bill!
Billy:	(*breaks away bashfully and hides behind tree*) Coo!
Daffy:	Billy! Where are you?
Billy:	(*Popping head out from behind tree*) Coo-eeee!
Daffy:	Come out, Billy. Don't waste time playing hide and seek.
Billy:	(*jumping out from behind tree*) Cuckoo!
Daffy:	(*fondly*) Silly Billy! Shall we sit down for a bit? There's a nice comfortable grassy bank over there. (*Leads him to it and they sit down*). The moon's beginning to rise—isn't it romantic?
Billy:	Aye!
Daffy:	Does it give you ideas?
Billy:	(*chuckles*) Oh ar!
Daffy:	Billy, have you ever been here in the company of another young lady?
Billy:	(*not committing himself*) Uh Huh!
Daffy:	Billy, have you ever been kissed?
Billy:	(*hedging*) Er—er—ar! (*Chuckles*) Oh, ar!
Daffy:	I'm sweet sixteen. Do you know what that means? (*Pause*) It means I never have—been kissed I mean.
Billy:	(*disbelieving*) Aw!
Daffy:	(*putting her face close to his*) Wouldn't you like to kiss me?
Billy:	(*bashfully*) Eeeeeh!
Daffy:	Go on. Do!
Billy:	Aw!
Daffy:	(*grabbing him*) Oh you gorgeous beast! (*Kisses him violently*) Mmmmmmmmm!
Billy:	(*falling back exhausted*) Oooooooooh! Er!
Daffy:	My cave man, my hero, love of my life!
Billy:	(*bashfully*) Aw!
Daffy:	Tell me you love me. (*Pause*) You do, don't you, Billy? Just a teeny weeny bit?
Billy:	Ar!

ACT TWO   THE HAPPY WIZARD

Daffy: My Billy! You say the nicest things.
Billy: (*equably*) Uh huh!
Daffy: Then that's settled. Tomorrow we'll go and see the vicar about putting up the banns next Sunday, and then we can be married before the end of the month. Won't that be wonderful? (*Pause*) Billy! Say something.
Billy: (*Takes a deep breath*) No!
Daffy: (*gives him a push and springs to her feet*) You great hulking brute! Casanova! You vile deceiver of innocent maidens! How could you say all those lovely things to me when all the time you were telling lies! You lead me to believe that you loved me—that your intentions were honourable when all the time you were laughing and taking advantage of a young girl's simplicity just to satisfy your masculine vanity. You—you—philanderer—how dare you trifle with my affections! A golden tongued snake in the grass, that's what you are.
I'm lucky to have found you out in time. (*With great dignity*) Now you may take me home and after you have kissed me goodnight on the doorstep I shall never speak to you again as long as I live. Come along, you! (*Takes him by the ear and leads him off right*).
Billy: (*as he goes*) Eeeeeeeh!
Felix: (*emerging from the shadows*) (*laughing*) If that is the normal behaviour of a woman in love it only strengthens my determination to remain a bachelor.
Hilarius: (*following and muttering to himself*) I knew Dewdrop's modern methods wouldn't work, and nothing I can say will convince this obstinate young man that there are girls, and *girls*.
Felix: What was that you said? Lately you seem to have developed a bad habit of muttering into your beard.
Hilarius: It was nothing of importance, I was just reminding myself of something Dewdrop told me to do.
Felix: Nothing she might say could be important. Speaking of fairies reminds me that we haven't seen anything of Discord for some time. Could he have lost interest in our doings?
Hilarius: That isn't likely; but he is not around quite so often as he used to be—the universal five day week, you know. Shorter hours, longer tea breaks and all that nonsense.

Felix:	That gives us breathing space. Does the shorter working week apply to Dewdrop?
Hilarius:	Oh no. She is conscientious. She likes overtime and even night duty.
Felix:	She would. (*Pause*) You know, Hilarius, I am beginning to feel really worried about Augustus. Despite his condescending manner he is apt to be timid when faced with physical danger and I am afraid he may have met with an accident. I propose we form a two man search party.
	(*Dewdrop pops out from her hiding place and unseen by Felix makes frantic signals to Hilarius*).
Hilarius:	(*cottoning on*) I don't think that would be altogether wise. One of us should stay. If he turns up and finds the mill deserted he may start looking for us. You stay and I will search the forest.
Felix:	Then take care. Good luck go with you. (*He turns towards the mill*).
Hilarius:	(*turning to go off right*) I will. I will. (*Sally enters right and looks round wearily*).
Hilarius:	Here's Sally. Splendid! Now perhaps things will start to happen.
	(*Sally turns abruptly and almost collides with him*).
Sally:	Mr. Wizard! I am so glad to see you. Will you please give this cloak to your friend—he left it in the tea garden.
Hilarius:	I'm sorry but I don't think I can spare the time. A pressing engagement, you know. I can't stop. Give it to him yourself. He's over there by the mill, Budgye my dear. (*He turns and bustles out right. Felix who has been leaning against the mill door suddenly sees Sally*).
Felix:	And what are you doing here, Miss Sally Lunn?
Sally:	(*haughtily*) I have as much right to be here as yourself. As a matter of fact you left your cloak at the tea garden. I came here to return it and for no other reason.
Felix:	How did you know where to find me?
Sally:	Our handyman overheard you making arrangements to meet your friends at the mill.
Felix:	Confounded spy.
Sally:	Don't be ridiculous. That simpleton a spy? Either you have too vivid an imagination or a guilty conscience.

ACT TWO   THE HAPPY WIZARD

And if that is the way you show gratitude for a good turn I'm sorry I bothered. (*Dumps cloak in Felix' arms*).

(*Fairy Dewdrop emerges from behind a tree, takes aim and fires as Sally turns on heel to go*).

Sound Effects Cue 18

Felix: (*clapping hand to forehead*) Oh!
Sally: (*pausing*) What's the matter?
Felix: Nothing. I think I've been bitten by a mosquito.
Sally: I can't see any blood.
Dewdrop: (*softly*) Bother! Missed the vital spot. (*Takes aim and fires again. Felix clutches his chest and starts to reel*).

Sound Effects Cue 19

Felix: Oh! (*He staggers*).
Dewdrop: A bull's eye! Well done Dewdrop old girl! (*Exit right taking gun and bag of equipment with her*).
Sally: (*impatiently*) What's the matter now? Another gnat bite?
Felix: I don't know. I've a pain in my chest and now I'm beginning to feel very dizzy. I am going to faint. Help me. Please.
Sally: You had better sit down on this bank and rest. (*She helps him to bank and he sits down, Sally kneels and he rests his head on her shoulder*).
Felix: My knees feel as if they are made of jelly and there's a golden haze in front of my eyes and roses, beautiful scented red roses are blooming everywhere.
Sally: You are delirious!
Felix: (*with satisfaction*) Yes. It's nice.
Sally: (*suspiciously*) Is this an act? Are you trying to make a fool of me?
Felix: How could you think such a thing? I feel very peculiar and my head is so hot. (*Sally rests her hand on his forehead*) That's lovely. Don't take your hand away.
Sally: (*a trifle worried now*) You certainly have got a temperature. I don't quite know what to do—I should be getting back home for Aunt Penny will start worrying if I am out after sunset; and yet I don't like leaving you here in this state. I must go and find help.

Felix:	*(firmly)* No. It's not safe to leave me alone. *(Pathetically)* I might die, solitary and friendless, and years might pass before anyone discovers my bleached white bones. Stay with me until my friends return, please do.
Sally:	*(reluctantly).* Very well. I will stay until you are feeling a little better or until someone comes.
Felix:	*(enjoying the situation)* Good. It may be a long time before I feel stronger and very few people pass this way. *(Sighs happily)* Isn't it a beautiful evening?
Sally:	*(a little puzzled)* It's very seasonable for June, but I am afraid there is more than a hint of thunder in the air.
Felix:	Don't let's talk about the weather. Tell me about yourself instead.
Sally:	There is very little to tell. Since my parents died, I've lived with Aunt Penelope helping her, rather unsuccessfully I am afraid, to run the village tea garden. But you know most of that anyway. I am just an ordinary girl.
Felix:	No, that's not true. You are anything but ordinary. *(Sits up and puts a tentative arm round Sally's shoulders).*
Sally:	*(evading the arm)* Obviously you are feeling much better. I will go now.
Felix:	Don't go yet. I might have a relapse, in fact I think I am going to now. *(Sinks back)* Put your arm round my shoulder for support, just in case I faint. That's much better.

Music Cue 17

Now apropos of what I was saying about your not being ordinary. You are very different from all the other girls I have met. Not only do you have beauty, but wit, courage and vivacity too. You are like a breath of fresh air. *(Song).*

Music Cue 18

BREATH OF FRESH AIR

You're like a breath of fresh air,
Somehow quite diff'rent, refreshingly rare,
Sweet as a morning in May,
Bright and elusive, enchantingly gay.

You're like the sparkle in wine
Yet cool as a forest of larches and pine;
Fresh as a midsummer breeze
Teasing so gently the leaves on the trees.

My life was lonely and sad
'til you came along yesterday,
Now I am happy and glad,
I'm walking on air all the way.

You swept the shadows away,
Leaving the sunshine instead of the grey;
Now all the outlook's set fair
Since you came along like a breath of fresh air.

Sally: (*with exaggerated politeness*) A very pretty compliment, kind sir.
Felix: Do you not approve of compliments?
Sally: Yes, when they happen to be sincere, but your pretty speech was obviously well practised. Indeed I think you must be the prince of platitudinarians.
Felix: Have you been borrowing from Augustus' vocabulary?
Sally: Certainly not. I have been to school even though I am but a peasant.
Felix: That I never doubted for one moment, your having been to school, I mean. But tell me, Sally, while we are on the subject of princes . . . .
Sally: I used the word prince merely as a figure of speech.
Felix: But of course. Are you yet betrothed or are you still waiting for your own particular prince to come along and carry you off on a white charger?
Sally: I don't see that it is any of your business, but the answer to both questions happen to be no.
Felix: I have been under the impression that every girl dreams of being courted and won by a handsome prince.
Sally: Not this girl. That kind of thing only goes on in fairy stories. I never have believed in the rags to riches Cinderella saga.
Felix: You puzzle me. I can't understand you.
Sally: Don't bother to try. The man who can understand a woman has yet to be born.

Felix: Do you really mean all you say? Seriously now, wouldn't you like to be given the opportunity of marrying a prince, or maybe someone of even higher rank?

Sally: (*scornfully*) Such a ridiculous situation is hardly likely to arise: and in any event, a marriage between two people from opposite ends of the social scale could never be anything but disastrous.

Felix: Why?

Sally: Because the relatives of both parties would have the strongest objections to the parties marrying outside their own class. And try to imagine the complications which would arise should there be children of such a marriage.

Felix: What complications?

Sally: They would follow the unfortunate example of their parents. The young princesses would fall in love with swineherds or the seventh sons of woodcutters and the princes with goosegirls or equally unsuitable persons and then the whole unsatisfactory business would start all over again. It could not possibly succeed. So if I marry, which is most unlikely, it will be to someone as ordinary as myself.

Felix: Sally, I did not think you were a snob, but you are even worse, you are an inverted snob.

Sally: (*getting up and walking away*) You don't know what you are talking about.

Felix: (*firmly*) Oh yes I do, and I haven't yet finished with the subject. You have not taken love into account and that would make all the difference in the world. What would you do if you were to fall in love with a prince?

Sally: That will never happen. I have no time for princes.

Felix: (*rising*) How do you know when you have never met one?

Sally: Oh yes I have! I met one at a party given by Queen Tryphena for the children of the palace servants. Prince Felix was the host, a beastly spoiled little boy who teased all the little girls. He pulled dreadful faces and put out his tongue. He had a very long tongue. Bright pink.

Felix: If you were as provoking then as you are now I can well understand his behaviour.

Sally: Oh you . . . . you . . . . you . . . .

ACT TWO   THE HAPPY WIZARD

Felix: *(laughing)* Sally Lunn, actually at a loss for words.
Sally: There you go with another ridiculous cliché. You are rude and conceited and I dislike you.
Felix: And you are behaving just like a woman.
Sally: I am not.
Felix: *(smiling in an infuriating way)* Have it your own way then. I don't really know why I bother to argue with you.
Sally: *(furiously)* Because you like the sound of your own voice, your majesty, you still talk too much and your tongue is still too long.
Felix: It is not. Look. *(He puts out his tongue at her)* And now I recognise you too. You are the horrid little girl who wore a pink frilly dress and pushed my face into a dish of cream trifle.
Sally: You only got what you deserved. What could you expect after hitting me on the head with a sausage roll?
Felix: I remember it quite clearly now, and I was very sorry afterwards.
Sally: *(amazed)* You? Sorry?
Felix: *(ruefully)* Yes. It was the last of the sausage rolls and I was still hungry.
Sally: *(stamping foot)* You are impossible and I would do it again if there were a trifle handy.
Felix: *(teasing)* Typically feminine. When a woman loses her temper and cannot think of anything bad enough to say she starts looking for something to throw.
(Sally grabs a lump of turf from the bank and hurls it at Felix. To her surprise it hits him. She takes a step backwards)
Sally: Oh, your majesty . . . . . .
Felix: Yes, Miss Sally Lunn, this time you have gone too far and you are going to get what you deserve. *(He seizes her by the shoulders and kisses her very thoroughly. Sally breaks away and slaps his face hard as Hilarius emerges from the trees. He steps quickly between them).*
Hilarius: What is all this about? Really Sally Lunn, nice girls do no behave in this fashion. Do you realise that you have just fetched His Imperial Majesty King Felix of Mythuanian a right fourpenny one? Oh dear! Now what have I said. I am so sorry. Master Felix, I've given away your identity.

THE HAPPY WIZARD ACT TWO

Felix: Not to worry, Hilarius. Sally knows who I am. (*To Sally*) Incidentally, how did you find out?
Sally: Quite simply. One—the royal cipher on your cloak! two—the proclamation! three—your arrogant and overbearing manner! As I said a moment ago, you have changed very little over the years. I am not ashamed of speaking the truth.
Felix: Well Sally, if that's the way you really feel and wish to get your own back all you have to do is to contact the palace guard, turn me in and collect the five hundred gold pieces offered in reward. It should be sufficient to solve all your financial problems.
Sally: I wouldn't take a penny of it if I were destitute. And as for the second part of the reward—I wouldn't touch you with a barge pole. So you need have no fear that I shall give you away. I cannot be bothered. And now may I take leave of your majesty? (*Curtsies with mock politeness*).
Felix: You may. But rest assured we shall meet again.
Sally: If so it will be none of my doing. (*Curtsies and hurries out*).
Felix: (*looking after her*). What a spitfire! Isn't she marvellous? So much more attractive than all those insipid milk and water princesses my mother trots out as prospective brides. (*Thoughtfully*) Hilarius, does it not strike you as ironic that the only girl to whom I have ever been attracted has not the least interest in me?
Hilarius: Destiny works in strange ways, sire.
Felix: (*sadly*) She never wants to see me again.
Hilarius: (*patting Felix on the shoulder*) You can safely ignore that. Women have a strange but predictable habit of changing their minds.
Felix: Are you sure?
Hilarius: Oh yes. (*Reminiscently*) In my youth I knew a pretty young witch . . . . . but that is another story. (*Looks keenly at Felix*) Are you alright, sir?
Felix: I think so, but just before you arrived I felt most peculiar as if I were quite intoxicated in fact. And I found myself saying the strangest things to that girl, asking her opinion on such vital matters as the possible success of a marriage between king and

ACT TWO　　　THE HAPPY WIZARD

	commoner. Do you know I found myself on the verge of proposing. I must be mad—me a misogamist.
Hilarius:	A hater of marriage. But not any longer?
Felix:	Not where Sally is concerned. She's one in a million and I only wish she could feel the same way about me. (*Leans against tree trunk and gazes at the moon*).
Hilarius:	(*aside*) Oh dear! The poor lad's got it badly but Sally seems to be a hard case. I knew Dewdrop was going the wrong way about things. I told her so. Now Master Felix, fly's timing, I mean time's flying and we must not stand here wasting it.
Felix:	(*pulling himself together*) I agree. Now it is more important than ever to find Harmony quickly, the alternative is too horrible to contemplate. And it is essential to put aside all thoughts of Sally—a difficult undertaking, but I need all my powers of concentration for the task in hand.
Hilarius:	And we musn't forget your friend Augustus. I want him here before Penelope comes, I mean before midnight. You go and look for him along the highway. I will remain here for a while.
Felix:	Very well, but if I have no luck before reaching the village I will come back here. Expect me in about an hour. (*Exit right*).
Hilarius:	Now to contact Dewdrop and find out why Sally has not responded to treatment. (*Chants*) 　　　Dewdrop, Dewdrop can you hear? 　　　Wizard calling, come in dear. (*number unobtainable sound*).

Sound Effects Cue 20

　　　　　　No reply, I'll try again. (*He does so and Dewdrop enters, out of breath*).

Sound Effects Cue 21

Dewdrop:	Sorry to be late but I had to go back to the heart clinic for some more darts and serum. Had to use both mine on Felix. The first shot went wide, but the next one was dead on target though, a bull's eye straight through the heart. I had to make absolutely sure the second time.

Hilarius: Do you mean that you gave that poor boy a double dose?
Dewdrop: Couldn't be helped. It won't hurt him. His was the worst case of misogamy I've ever encountered. But not to worry, I've never lost a love match yet.
Hilarius: You haven't had much experience!
Dewdrop: How did he react?
Hilarius: Violently. But you will have to do something about Sally. She's hopping mad with him—slapped his face when he kissed her.
Dewdrop: (*with interest*) That's a very good sign.
Hilarius: (*puzzled*) Sign of what?
Dewdrop: That she is half in love with him already.
Hilarius: (*bewildered*) Then why did she hit him?
Dewdrop: Reflex action. Although she thought she hated him, she really wanted him to kiss her, and when he did she thoroughly enjoyed it, and that's why she got so furious. It's the automatic reaction of a woman's built-in emotional defence mechanism.
Hilarius: Excuse me if I seem a little bit dim but your diagnosis is quite beyond me You are trying to blind me with science
Dewdrop: No I am not. It's simple feminine logic.
Hilarius: That's worse.
Dewdrop: Rubbish! Even a little girl could understand it. Now I can't waste time chatting, must be off to give Sally her injection. Bye bye. I'll look in again later unless you want me urgently. You have my number, haven't you. Bye! (*Picks up bag and exit right*).
Hilarius (*sits down on bank*). She gets more frighteningly efficient every time I see her, but I still don't altogether trust her new fangled methods. I may be an old been has, no, has been of an old wizard but my elixirs and dizzy aphrodisiacs still work very well and they are so much more romantic. Her ways are so clinical: I don't know what the world is coming to, I really don't. What with . . . .
Felix: (*dashing in*) I have found Augustus, but he is in the most shocking state of mind. That dreadful Penny Bunn seems to have him completely under her thumb and he does not seem to mind. They are heading this way. Hilarius, we must do something to rescue him from her clutches. Put on your thinking cap.

Hilarius: I can't. It's at home in Harmony.
Felix: And a fat lot of good it is to us there.
Hilarius: Not to worry. I have a feeling fate is on our side.

Sound Effects Cue 22

Felix: (*angrily*) Don't be so inanely cheerful and smug about it. If you could only see him, it's pathetic. Oh, I can hear them coming.
(*Penelope enters mounted precariously on Nelly and holding a stick from which dangles a carrot. Augustus pushes Nelly from behind. He smiles foolishly from time to time*).
Penny: Giddy yup, Nelly. Come along old girl. We are almost there. Give her another push, Gussie. That's better. Whoa now! Steady girl!
Felix: Gussie indeed. Did you hear that, Hilarius?
Hilarius: Yes, yes. (*Softly*) It's worked!
Felix: Augustus, what do you think you are doing? You are well aware of our predicament, so why have you brought this woman here?
Augustus (*loftily*) I encountered this sweet damsel by the wayside and in dire distress. Her mount had collapsed, and the least I could do was to offer my humble services in such an emergency.
Felix: (*sighing*) What happened?
Penny: Nelly be not used to being ridden by a lady and her back end gave way. But Gussie here were wonderful, he knowed just what to do and we were on our way again in next to no time. Help me dismount please. (*Augustus does so and she walks stiffly away from Nelly*) I be right glad to be back on what Gussie calls terra firma. (*Looks round*) Why, we all be together again. This be so nice.
Felix: (*taking Augustus aside*) I still don't understand why you had to bring Miss Penelope here.
Augustus Because the old mill happens to be her destination.
Penny: That reminds me, one of the reasons for coming here was to give this old stick back to Mr. Hilarius. You left it on the table, sir. (*Hands wand to wizard*).
Hilarius: Thank you, Miss Bunn. How silly of me to leave it lying about. (*Chuckles*) I must be getting forgetful in my old age.

Felix: There's more in this than meets the eye. What are you up to?
Hilarius: Nothing, nothing at all.
Penny: (*looking round*) But where's my Sally? Daffy told me she was supposed to be coming here.
Felix: She left here about ten minutes ago. Didn't you pass her on the way?
Penny: I didn't notice anyone as I were occupied with other things. I'd best go and catch her up and bring her back with me. I'll ride Nelly, she's a right turn of speed when she's a mind to go fast. I won't be long.
Felix: Madam, when you catch up with her I think you should go home. It is very late and there may be a storm.
Penny: No, I'll come back. I've some wonderful news and I want us all to be together when I tell it. Cheery Bye. (*Leads Nelly off stage*).
Felix: Thank goodness! I thought we should never get rid of her. Come along Augustus, we must be away by the time she returns.
Augustus: (*with great dignity*) You may go, but I shall remain. That woman, as you so rudely called Miss Penelope, is a lady of inestimable worth. She is a fountain of kindness, and when I came upon her, so dignified in her distress, she, in her generosity insisted on sharing with me her own repast—jam butties and elderberry wine. Truly an epicurean feast. At the very mention of her name I seem to be enveloped in a roseate glow. (*Smiles fatuously*).
Felix: You are indeed ill, my old friend. Hilarius, he is out of his mind. What can we do?
Hilarius: Nothing really. He is suffering from the effects of the elix . . . elderberry wine. Home made wine can be potent and he is unused to it.
Felix: We can't go on while Augustus is in this state. Help me get him into the mill: a good rest will, to put it bluntly, help to sober him up. (*They half carry the bemused Augustus into the mill*).
(*Penny re-enters on foot, dragging a reluctant Sally by the hand*).
Sally: Aunt Penny, why do you want to come back here? It's late and I want to go home. I'm tired and miserable.

ACT TWO — THE HAPPY WIZARD

Penny: Nonsense. You be just unsettled. It be the Spring, and all folks be affected differently, some falls in love and some comes out in spots. A good dose of brimstone and treacle in the morning will soon put you right.
Sally: If you don't stop treating me like a child I shall scream.
Penny: You do be sickening for something, that's for sure.
Sally: I am not. Take me home before those play-acting friends of yours return.
Penny: Play-acting? You don't think they be strolling players do you?
Sally: Don't you know who they really are? You heard that proclamation. The young man is none other than His Majesy King Felix of Mythuania amusing himself at the expense of the peasantry, only do not say anything to anyone because I promised, and goodness knows why, not to give him away.
Penny: But Gussie—who be my Gussie?
Sally: Your Gussie is none other than his majesty's erstwhile tutor, the Archduke Augustus.
Penny: (*sinking down on bank*) Oh my! I thought he be someone special, but I never dreamed he would turn out to be a titled gentleman. Oh goodness! Just fancy plain Penny Bunn mixing with the quality. Oh dear! I wish I were young and beautiful and a real lady.
Sally: Dear Aunt Penny you are a lady and I don't want you to be any different from what you are now.
Penny: But Gussie, His Grace I mean, seems to like me and despite his hoity toity ways he'd be quite a gay dog if I gave him a lead. (*Giggles*).
Sally: You are talking a lot of nonsense and saying the kind of things one expects to hear from Daffy. It's not like you. What is the matter?
Penny: You will know, all in good time.
Sally: For heaven's sake tell me now.
Penny: Later.
Sally: Then it will have to be much later. I am going home.
Penny: You can't. I've arranged to sell the teagarden to Billy and Daffy. The deeds be signed and sent off by pigeon post.

Sally: If this is your idea of a joke then I think it's very unfunny.
Penny: It's quite true but don't you worry your pretty little head about it. Everything in the garden is lovely. You'll see. *(Sally weeps)* Now what be the matter?
Sally: I haven't got a home to go to and I'll never see Felix again.
Penny: I thought you didn't like that young man?
Sally: I don't, in fact I hate him—I think. And now I'm not only an orphan but a waif and stray as well, thanks to you.
Penny: *(going to her)* There be nothing to cry about love. It'll all come right in the end, you'll see. Now dry your eyes while I go and find the others. I expect they be only in the mill. *(Goes into mill, leaving Sally looking disconsolate. She stands, leaning back on a tree trunk).*

Music Cue 19

Sally: *(to herself)* What a horrible mess. We are homeless, unemployed and Aunt Penny's behaving like a silly schoolgirl with a secret. As for myself I am so mixed up I don't know where I am or what to think and I cannot see any way out of it all. *(Song).*

Music Cue 20

THERE'LL BE NO HAPPY ENDING

There'll be no happy ending,
It's no use
Pretending
Otherwise.

There'll be no happy meeting
No gay word
Of greeting
Just goodbyes.

And all because I uttered words
I didn't mean to say.
I'm broken hearted 'cause I threw
My happiness away.

> There'll be no bright tomorrow,
> And sorrow
> No blue skies
> Just sadness
>
> No happy ever after
> No gladness
> No laughter
> Only sighs.

Verse:
> I don't know how it happened,
> Or by what trick of fate,
> I failed to recognise love
> Until it was too late.

(*As Sally finishes her song a strange little procession emerges from the mill. Sally looks apprehensive*).

Penny: (*shyly*). Will you be making the announcement, Gussie?

Augustus (*dropping on one knee before Felix*) Sire, I crave your gracious permission to enter into the state of matrimony with Miss Bunn.

Felix: (*aghast*) Augustus, did I hear rightly that you and this person . . . . . .

Augustus Indeed sire, it is true.

Felix: This news comes as a tremendous shock for I had no idea you were contemplating marriage with anyone, least of all with this . . . . this lady. How and when did you come to this decision?

Augustus: I know not the exact hour, but at the very same moment this lady and I discovered we were mutually attracted. Have I your leave to pay my addresses to her?

Felix: I only hope you fully realise what you are doing. Yes Augustus, you have our formal permission (*raises Augustus and shakes him by the hand*) Congratulations and our good wishes.

(*Penny drops a clumsy curtsy and Hilarius bustles forward*).

Hilarius: My felicitations too. I do hope you will be happy. Miss Ha'penny.

Penny: Penny, please. I be not one for doing things by halves.

Felix:		Augustus, have you given thought as to how my mother will react to such news? You know well her habit of throwing the harbingers of er—unusual tidings headlong into the dungeons.
Augustus		*(with hauteur)* If the royal lady likes it not she can lump it. *(Bows hurriedly)* With respect, of course.
Felix:		You have changed. Either you are intoxicated or out of your tiny mind.
Penny:		*(indignantly)* He be neither. Sorry your Majesty, I didn't mean no harm but nobody's going to say nasty things about my Gussie. I be so happy I don't know whether I be on my head or my heels; there be so many arrangements to be made, my dresses to be ordered and my bottom drawers. Sally, my love, you will be your old aunt's bridesmaid, won't you. *(Sally slips away into the shadows).* Sally! Where be you going? *(Goes after her and brings her down stage).*
Sally:		You won't be needing me now. I will go away somewhere and start a new life.
Penny:		Nonsense! You will make your home with Gussie and me after the wedding. I can hardly believe it, plain Penny Bunn living in a small castle and mixing in high society. I shall give balls and receptions and invite lots of nice young men to partner you. I can see it all.
Sally·		I can't. But thank you all the same. If the Archduke has no objections I will stay with you for a little while until I find suitable work to do.
Felix:		Sally, after your aunt's wedding she will be received at court, so no doubt you and I will meet again. So may we not be friends?
Sally:		If your majesty so commands.
Felix:		I do not command you, Sally. I am asking you.
Sally:		*(coldly)* Very well. It shall be as your majesty wishes.
Hilarius:		When is the wedding to be, Miss Penny Farthing? No, that's a bicycle. Miss Penny Bunn?
Penny:		In three days' time. I always had a secret yearning to elope, but Gussie said not as it wouldn't be quite proper for a man of his station. *(Wistfully)* But it would have been exciting.
Felix:		You did say that the wedding was to be in three days' time?

ACT TWO THE HAPPY WIZARD

Hilarius: Master Felix, do not be dismayed by this turn of events. Do you not realise what it means? If Miss Penny is already mar........

Felix: Great Heavens! Yes! Penny and Augustus will be married before the time limit expires and even Discord cannot compel her to be a bigamist.

Sally: Aunt Penny a bigamist? What nonsense is this?

Felix: (*hedging*) That's just what it is—nonsense, I mean. It all stems from a ridiculous wager I made with a rascally demon when I was in a tight spot. There is no need for you to worry your pretty head about it because the conditions no longer apply.

Lighting Cue 27

Sound Effects Cue 23

(*There is a flash and a roll of thunder as Discord appears left clad in a suit of shining black armour*).

Discord: Nothing is changed, my friend. So you thought you could foil Discord with your stupid little plot. Such an assumption is premature and the bargain still stands.

Sally: What bargain is this?

Penny: Please explain.

Discord: Have they not told you now? Can it be that the noble king and his honourable friends have kept you in the dark? Shame on them. But it will give me much pleasure to enlighten you. That conceited young coxcomb had the nerve to defy me—me, Discord, doyen of all demons. Of course I could have despatched him there and then, but I dislike killing. I prefer a more sophisticated type of punishment designed specifically to afford the greatest prolonged misery to each individual victim.

Penny: How be I concerned?

Discord: Our friend over there (*points to Felix*) challenged my right to the lost kingdom of Harmony. I made him a fair offer—if he finds it within seven days he can restore it to Hilarius. If he fails he will have to endure a lifetime of misery and woe. A life sentence in the form of marriage to the first woman he encountered after the conclusion of our deal. A perfect punishment for a marriage hater. Could you devise a better?

THE HAPPY WIZARD ACT **TWO**

Sally: And that woman happens to be Aunt Penny? There must be another way out, for my aunt's sake.
Felix: There is. I intend finding that kingdom within the given time. Trust me, Sally.
Sally: I don't care about you. My concern is for Aunt Penny's future. How could you be a party to such a stupid bargain? Why didn't you fight? You have a most expensive looking sword or is it just a fashion accessory?
Discord: My dear young lady he had no option. The sword of a mortal is powerless against my magic.
Felix: If you had tumbled out of the book, Sally, how different it would have been.
Sally: A fine knight errant you have proved yourself to be. The more I see of you the more I dislike you. You, a strong young man, a reigning monarch, and still tied to your mother's apron strings. You are nothing but a puppet, a cardboard king.
Discord: Bravo! young lady. But to return to the business in hand; in order to protect my interests I had better take care of Miss Bunn for the next few days.
Augustus: (*frightened, but making an effort*) The damsel is my betrothed. Touch her not.
Discord: So you defy me, you pathetic little pedant? Either you are very brave or very stupid. But I will give you the benefit of the doubt and let you prove your worth. We will duel for the lady.
Penny: No, no.
Augustus: (*to Felix*) Will you act as my second?
Felix: Certainly not. You are completely ignorant in the art of duelling. I will be your champion and fight in your stead.
Augustus: No, thank you sire. I will fight my own battle. Penny, may I have the temporary loan of your horse?
Felix: Stop being an idiot, you have never ridden in your life and would be unhorsed before you had time to couch a lance.
Augustus: Your Majesty forgets I have seen service in the lancers.
Felix: Surely not in my time. When did you leave the regiment?
Augustus: (*awkwardly*) Well, I was mixed up in the wrong set and banished from the ballroom.

ACT TWO THE HAPPY WIZARD

Discord: As a concession to your inexperience, little scholar, we will fight on foot and you may choose your weapons.
Sally: He is a brave little man but he has neither weapons nor armour. The outcome is a foregone conclusion. It is not fair.
Discord: It is a demon's prerogative to be unfair.
Penny: (*goes to Hilarius*) Please wave your wand and conjure up some armour for my Gussie.
Hilarius: It shall be done. (*Waves wand and chants*).
 Abra cadabra, riddle me ree,
 Tun tiddley um tum, fi fum fo fee!

Sound Effects Cue 24

Lighting Cue 28

(*Nelly enters harnessed to a wheelbarrow which contains a large box*).
There you are Miss Penny Weight, sent by carrier too. No doubt it is a panoply fit for a paladin.
Felix: (*goes to barrow and opens box*) Let us see. Now what have we here? (*Pulls out large saucepan*) Is this a helmet? (*Brings out dustbin lid*) and this a shield? (*Rummages about*) There's everything here including the kitchen stove, but nothing like a suit of armour.
Hilarius: Dearie dearie me! I've made a stew, no, a hash of things again. Perhaps if I were to try again . . . . . ?
Discord: Sorry, you have had your chance. Come little dominie, don your accoutrements.
Felix: (*going to Augustus*) We shall have to make the best of things and pray that fate is on our side. Will you not change your mind and let me take your place? In fact I command you to do so.
Augustus: I never thought to see the day when I would openly defy the sovereign's command. But honour takes precedence. I cannot and will not be a coward. Help me prepare for combat.

(*Discord draws his sword and practises up stage left while the others help Augustus dress up in the kitchen equipment. A breast plate is a tray, oven gloves are gauntlets, a feather duster the sword, etc. He takes up position in centre stage, the four spectators move down stage right. Hilarius puts an arm round Sally*

	on one side and round Penny on the other. *Felix Stands slightly apart, his hand on the hilt of his sword*).
Augustus:	I am ready.
Penny:	Just a moment. (*Discreetly removes garter*) **Wear** this as a good luck token in your helmet. (*Ties it on saucepan handle*).
Augustus:	(*shocked*) Miss Penelope, you go too far, even for this permissive age.
Felix:	Nonsense. You must wear your lady's gage. Where is your sense of chivalry?
Augustus:	I am ready
Discord:	(*taking up position*) En garde!
Hilarius:	Then let battle commence.
Penny:	Which one be battle?
All:	Be quiet!

Music Cue 21

> (*slowly the protagonists circle to the strains of a waltz. Occasionally they thrust and parry, Augustus, by some miracle evading Discord's thrusts. Occasionally the former's feather duster finds its mark, evoking a giggle from Discord. The tempo quickens and Penny, unable to contain herself any longer, seizes a toasting fork from the box and hurls herself into the fray. She shuts her eyes and aims blindly at the gyrating bodies, catching Augustus squarely in the seat*).

Penny: (*triumphantly*) Once more into the breach!

Music Cue 22

> (*The music stops abruptly as Agustus falls flat on his face*).

Discord:	My victory, I think.
Penny:	(*sobbing*) Poor darling Gussie—be you dead?
Augustus:	Yes.
Hilarius:	(*feels Augustus' heart*) He is still breathing.
Penny:	Then stop him, somebody.
Augustus:	I think I am alive, but not very well.

ACT TWO　　　　THE HAPPY WIZARD

Discord: A pity the fight had to end in such an undignified manner. My grateful thanks to you, Miss Penny, for your invaluable assistance. Now I think you had better come with me. I will release you in a few days in good time for your wedding with the king. (*Bows mockingly to Felix*).

Penny: I don't know who you be, but I think you be a nasty interfering old man. I am engaged to Gussie and I refuse to be married off to anybody else, king or no king.

Discord: Hold your tongue, woman.
(*Penny does so, literally*)

Sally: Are you all going to stand there and do nothing.
(*Before Felix can reply Discord swiftly touches Hilarius, Felix and the prone Augustus with the tip of his sword. They 'freeze'*).

Discord: They are now powerless to move or speak. I have bewitched them and thus they will remain until Miss Penny is safely hidden away.
(*Penny is making choking noises of protest*).
Well, woman. What are you blubbering about? I have not taken away your powers of speech.

Sally: Yes, you have. You told her to hold her tongue.

Discord: I'll brook no impertinence from a chit of a girl. I do not altogether trust you, so I will take you into custody with your aunt. In the next day or two you will have ample time to dwell on the pleasant prospects of having a handsome young uncle. (*Leers*).

Sally: No, not that.

Lighting Cue 18

Discord: Oh yes! (*Seizing Penny and Sally he drags them off stage left. Slowly the others stretch their muscles. They help Augustus to his feet*).

Felix: We are in a worse situation than ever and it is mainly my fault.

Augustus: No one is to blame. Discord is too clever for us.

Felix: No, in my position I must take full responsibility. I had vainglorious visions of myself as a swashbuckling dare devil. And what am I? Just a fool with big ideas.

THE HAPPY WIZARD ACT TWO

Hilarius: Non and stuffsense! Had it not been for you and Augustus where would I be now? Just bumbling along trying to find Harmony all by myself. And friendship means a great deal to a lonely old wizard, semi-retired. You must not get dumps in the down.

Sound Effects Cue 25
(Dewdrop enters from right to sound of harp music).

Dewdrop: Now what's all this about being down in the dumps? We can't have silly attitudes like this can we? I seem to have arrived at a time of crisis. *(notices Augustus seated on the bank, still wearing a stupified expression)* How long has he been like this?

Felix: For some considerable time.

Dewdrop: *(goes to him, dumps bag and feels his pulse)* Temperature high, patient perspiring profusely, heart beat phenomenal; eyes glazed and obviously moonstruck; breath coming in languorous sighs. Hm! Has he been behaving out of character?

Felix: Very much so.

Dewdrop: I thought as much. It's an acute attack of love sickness. There's a lot of it about. Has he been in contact with anyone beside yourselves?

Hilarius: *(warily)* Well, only Miss Penelope Bunn.

Dewdrop: She must be isolated without delay.

Felix: She can't be. Discord has kidnapped her together with her niece.

Dewdrop: I think I am beginning to understand. What part did you play in all this, Hilarius?

Hilarius: *(backing away)* Well, not very much really. I only thought I would try and help Felix, so I doctored the elderberry wine in order to . . . .

Dewdrop: Don't bother to explain, I can guess your motives. I ought to have known you wouldn't be able to resist meddling and messing things up. I just cannot imagine two victims so totally incompatible. Never mind though, there's no great harm done. These outdated elixirs have a very short lasting effect. The infatuation should wear off in a matter of hours and the patients will remember little or nothing of it. In fact I think I can speed matters up. *(Opens bag and takes out very large hypodermic).* An injection should do the trick.

ACT TWO   THE HAPPY WIZARD

Augustus: No, no, no!
Dewdrop: Don't be a baby! (*Augustus clutches his arms and turns away*) All right then, you can have a tablet instead, (*pops one in his mouth*) and here's a peppermint lump to take the taste away. He'll soon be himself again.
Felix: Thank goodness for that. The spectacle of my tutor behaving like a love sick calf was too awful for words. It will be good to see him normal again, and we need all our wits about us if we are to get out of this desperate situation.
Dewdrop: Look on the bright side. Have you forgotten that you still hold the key of friendship and trust? Think also of Augustus' brave effort in tackling Discord virtually unarmed. For that I shall award him this key of courage. (*Takes ribbon and key out of bag and hangs it round Augustus' neck*). And as for you, Felix, you haven't acquitted yourself with any great distinction as yet, but you have learned the secret of humility and for that you too may have a key. (*Hangs similar one round his neck*).
Now remember, faint heart never won fair lady as the saying goes. I'll be keeping an eye on the Archduke, but his progress should be normal from now on. (*Picks up bag*) Farewell! (*Exit right*).

Sound Effects Cue 26

Hilarius: Welfare, welfare!
Felix: She's very free with good advice but rather mean with practical help. Have you any bright ideas? All I can think of is Sally, helpless in the clutches of that rogue: but what to do about it I just do not know. How are you feeling, Augustus?
Augustus: (*sitting up right*) Where am I? Have I been indisposed?
Felix: You might call it that.
Augustus: How did I get here?
Felix: Never mind about that. You have had an unfortunate experience, but it is all behind you. However, there is one bit of good news—both you and I have acquired a further key, yours for courage and mine for . . . . this should amuse you, humility.
Augustus: It's coming back to me now, I am beginning to understand.

Hilarius: Understand what?
Augustus: It occurs to me that the keys we hold are of abstract human qualities, all of them excellent. Therefore if we are to obtain more, then we ourselves must acquire more of these traits.
Felix: You mean we should be goody goodies? What a dull prospect.
Augustus: Not necessarily so, sire. Already in the recent course of our adventures we have gained a certain amount of tolerance. Is not that, for instance, another admirable characteristic?
Hilarius: (*pointing upwards*) Look! Look! There's that pigeon again. He has dropped something. (*They all duck as a key drops from the flies*). Yes, it is a key. (*Picks it up*) It is labelled 'tolerance'.
Felix: If we add any more to the bunch it will weigh us down.
Augustus: A little less levity, please.
Felix: Careful! Do not lose the new found key of tolerance.
Hilarius: I think I know where there may be other keys, lots of them.
Felix: Where?
Hilarius: In the Realm of Music. My Kingdom of Harmony just might be there too.
Augustus: And probably Discord.
Felix: True. And Sally is with him. Come Augustus. (*Helps him to rise*) Which way do we go, Hilarius?
Hilarius: There are many ways. Down the Primrose Path, the Straight and Narrow Way, Uphill, Downdale, Middleway—which ever one you care to choose.
Felix: This may be some kind of test of endurance so we will take the difficult one, uphill. You will have to be our guide, Hilarius, I am lost.
Hilarius: Me too.
Augustus: Then it is largely your own fault!
Felix: Mine?
Augustus: Yes. Right at the beginning of this disastrous story you became what is known as a runaway character. You have run away with yourself, taking Hilarius and me with you, right from the point when you leapt through the cover of our book.

Felix: You have given me an idea. Why did I not think of it before? We will look in the book and it will tell us the way to the Realm of Music.
Hilarius: But we left the book behind us.

Music Cue 23

Felix: Oh no; we did not. I have the paper back edition in my pocket. (*Produces it and they skip off stage to the strains of BACK IN THE BOOK*).

Lighting Cue 30

Lighting Cue 31

BLACKOUT

Lighting Cue 32

Music Cue 24 (Entracte)

Lighting Cue 33

ACT III
Scene 1

The Realm of Music.

> This set uses about two thirds of the stage depth. Black velvet curtains mask the wings and a gauze, lighted from the front forms a back cloth. Behind this is concealed the original book set. Silver notes and white musical symbols and cut out instruments are appliquéd to the black drapes and gauze. There should be many of these thus providing plenty of glitter in contrast to the black curtains. Upstage right is a white five barred gate, the handle of which is shaped like a treble clef. Upstage left is a white painted kiosk, the window of which is closed. One or two upturned drums are placed about to provide seats. There is a tubular bell close to the gate.

Lighting Cue 34

> (*Felix, Hilarius and Augustus enter right and lean on the gate. All three seem weary*).

Music Cue 25

Felix: The Realm of Music at last. I never imagined when we set out that the journey would be so difficult. I hope it proves worth it.

Augustus: With all due respect, your majesty, how could you expect the journey to be otherwise? The book you brought along had two pages missing.

Hilarius: Never mind. We did find the way despite all the obstacles.

Felix: Well, Music is our last hope. Where else are we to look for Harmony, Discord and my Sally? How much time is left?

Augustus: Twelve hours, my liege.

Felix: Then we will invade this realm immediately, the defences appear to be negligible. (*Draws sword*). Stand back while I break the lock.

ACT THREE THE HAPPY WIZARD

Augustus: Desist, sire, I beg of you. The Queen Mother (*bows*) would be appalled by such uncouth behaviour. Would it not be more seemly to ring the bell and request admittance in the normal way?

Felix: You are right, old friend. In my desperation to find Sally common sense and good manners seem to have gone by the board. Thank you for bringing me back to my senses. (*Rings bell*).

Sound Effects Cue 27

(*Dr. Solfa enters left, a flamboyant character dressed in academic cap and gown and carrying a conductor's baton. He speaks with a slight Italian accent*).

Solfa: (*bowing*) Good morning, Gentlemen! You wish to enter?

Felix: If you please, kind sir.

Solfa: And your reason, young man?

Felix: We seek the Kingdom of Harmony and have reason for thinking it my be found within the confines of the Realm of Music.

Solfa: Harmony here? In this day and age? You must be joking.

Augustus: It seemed to be the obvious place to look.

Solfa: Then you are indeed behind the times. But please to enter—the gate is never locked as there are no barriers in the Realm of Music. It is an international settlement. May I have your names please, just for the visitors' book.

Felix: Felix, king of Mythuania, my companion, the Archduke Augustus and Hilarious, a wizard of renown.

Solfa: Hm! The occasion calls for the distinguished visitors' book. I am Dr. Solfa, custodian of this realm. At your service. (*bows*) Do come in, please. (*They go through gate*).

Hilarius: How do you do Doctor? I have heard much about your tonic. I must remember to buy a bottle next time I feel under the weather.

Augustus: The good doctor's degree is in music not medicine.

Hilarius: Do forgive me. I should have known better, but unfortunately I don't.

Felix: Your post of custodian carries great responsibility, no doubt?

THE HAPPY WIZARD   ACT THREE

Solfa: Indeed, and I am also registrar of births. We have no deaths, of course. Music goes on forever.
Felix: Who lives here?
Solfa: The brain children of all the world's composers.
Augustus: All of them? Then you too must be suffering a population explosion and consequent housing shortage?
Solfa: No, no, no. We have unlimited accommodation as every note has it own flat.
Felix: An ideal state.
Solfa: It used to be, but alas, not now. It all dates back from the time the modern composers, Bartok and Shostakovitch, to say nothing of the pop groups, who introduced Discord into Music. He's always been here unofficially, of course, but now they have made him a member and it has turned his head. There is trouble wherever he goes. There are always major or minor clashes going on everywhere and just recently there was a sharp encounter between the black notes and the white notes. It is most disturbing. Harmony as we knew it has gone forever.
Hilarius: Oh dear, Harmony was my kingdom too.
Felix: Don't despair, Hilarius. The musical side is only one part of Harmony and if we persevere we may help Dr. Solfa too. Where is Discord to be found?
Solfa: He is about somewhere, of that you may be sure. Miss Melody, my assistant, may be able to help you, she has many contacts. (*Goes to kiosk and knocks*) Miss Melody? Are you there? Yes? No. Evidently she has not yet arrived. The poor dear lives in one of the outlying districts and has quite a distance to travel. Local transport services to Ivory Novelloton are very poor these days.
Augustus: Ivory Novelloton?
Solfa: Have you not heard of it? It is the Budleigh Salterton of Ruritania whence all the exiled royalty of operetta retire. The population consists almost entirely of kings, queens, princes and the like, although there may be an odd count, countess or baron.
Felix: Very intriguing. There must be enough blue blood there to fill an ocean.
Solfa: Oh, there is, there is. And of course, every building is either a palace or a castle. It is the centre of gracious living.

ACT THREE THE HAPPY WIZARD

Augustus: Obviously. In your opinion, do you think we may find Harmony there?
Solfa: Only the ghost of Harmony. The Novelloton atmosphere is mainly one of brave melancholia. Ninety per cent of the royal couples married for convenience, political alliances, you understand. They renounced true love for love of their country. The real sweethearts of the kings and princes were midinettes or lovely daughters of innkeepers and the princesses' lovers were penniless music masters or brave junior officers.
Hilarius: (*wiping his eyes*) How very sad.
Solfa: Perhaps, but you would not think so if you saw them. Their heads are held high, upper lips are stiff and brave smiles are glued to their faces.
Felix: But what about the others?—The little milliners and the handsome captains. Did they marry someone of their own class in the course of time?
Solfa: No, no, no. They always remain faithful to their lost loves, but do not be concerned for these star crossed lovers, they glory in their nostalgia and popular musical comedy writers are indebted to them for inspiration.
Felix: I cannot help but be concerned. There is a parallel between those unhappy people and myself.
Hilarius: But we are characters in a fairy story and fairy stories always have happy endings.
Felix: So many unorthodox things have happened in this particular fairy story that I'm not counting on tradition. But I'm not yet in despair. Isn't it about time your assistant was here?
Solfa: (*goes to kiosk and knocks*) Miss Melody? (*The trap opens and Melody's head and shoulders appear. She is a sweet, faded lady, her voice soft and her manner deprecating and occasionally coy*).
So there you are at last, by dear. Was the traffic very bad?
Melody: Simply dreadful. At the junction of Memory Lane and Tin Pan Alley I ran into the most ghastly jam session you can imagine, and after sitting there for hours and hours I left my carriage and walked.
Solfa: Come out of the box office and talk to these gentlemen; they have a score to settle with your old enemy.

Melody: (*comes out from kiosk*) Discord? (*Dramatically*) He ruined my life. Fifty years ago I was the darling of the musical world; courted every night of the year; men sought my favours the world over; I was the glittering star of opera, concerts and balls; the toast of the capitals of the civilised world. Now I am just a forgotten melody, occasionally remembered in Palm Court on Sunday evenings.

Hilarius: (*wiping eyes*) So sad, so sad. I do sympathise.

Melody: Thank you, thank you. But I have my memories.

Solfa: (*impatiently*) Yes, yes, yes. Thank you Miss Melody. (*Aside to Felix*) She still tries to hog the limelight, you know and won't accept the fact that she's a back number.
Now Miss Melody, these gentlemen wish to find Discord prestissimo. Have you any idea where he may be disporting himself?

Melody: (*slightly offended*) Try the central European club— the Rhapsodies are usually congregated there. Noisy fellows they are, and Discord is on friendly terms with them. Their wild exuberance suits his mood.

Augustus: Thank you, madam. And where else do you seek our Demon.

Melody: (*still a little non-co-operative*) He may be anywhere in the wide world, or even the universe.

Hilarius: Oh dear! The universe is inaccessible to such mortals as my friends.

Solfa: Nonsense, my friend.

Augustus: I must concur with the statement of the wizard, he ...

Solfa: Your pardon, sir, but our great composer Gustav Holst made contact with the planets years ago. Any good orchestra will transport you there.

Felix: And if I must, I will journey to the ends of the earth to find Sally.

Music Cue 26

Augustus: (*Pointing down stage left*) My liege, take cover. There is a person slinking along in a manner most suspicious. Have a care, he looks like an assassin.

Lighting Cue 35

(*A black bearded sinister looking man in a wide brimmed black hat and voluminous black cloak and*

ACT THREE   THE HAPPY WIZARD

carrying a smoking bomb slinks furtively across the stage. He looks round slowly and menacingly then exit)

Felix: *(making ready to go)* I must follow him. He looks uncommonly like Discord in one of his disguises.

Solfa: *(detaining him)* No. Do not bother to go after him, I pray you. He is only M. Chopin's Revolutionary. He's a bit of a mystery, at best one of the cloak and dagger boys, and at the worst an assassin. I believe he is no more than a perpetual student. He's carried that bomb about for years, but it has never yet gone off.
If you remain here for a while you will see quite a number of musical personalities returning from concerts.

Felix: This is all very diverting, but we must be getting on with our search.

Hilarius: Yes, yes, we must be on our way. Come Felix, come Augustus. Come Hilarius. Now where's Hilarius— Oh, I am a stupid old thing. I'm Hilarius. I shall be forgetting my own name if I'm not careful. Now I'm sure there was something we had to ask the good doctor. Ah, yes, the keys. You have lots of keys, Dr. Solfa, perhaps one of them might open the door to Harmony.

Solfa: *(shakes head)* Somehow I doubt it. Indeed, I have many—A major, B flat minor, C sharp; you may examine them all. Come with me into the music library.

Felix: Augustus, you go with Dr. Solfa, you too, Hilarius. I think I will take a walk in this strange land and reconnoitre.

Solfa: As you please, King Felix, although I don't think you will have far to look for Discord. You may well hear him long before you see him for he is very fond of blowing his own trumpet—fortissimo.

Felix: Point taken. And I am ready to face the music.
Solfa: Counterpoint taken!
Felix: How dark it grows!

Lighting Cue 36

Solfa: The Fugues are about—rather gloomy creatures, but quite harmless.

Augustus: I like it not. My newly acquired bravado is rapidly evaporating.
Felix: Then go with Dr. Solfa and Melody. You will not come to any harm in their presence.
(Solfa, Melody, Augustus and Hilarius go out down stage left. Felix is left standing centre stage).
Felix: Now what? I suppose I could call in Dewdrop, I don't like doing it, but I can't think of anything else. I wonder if I can remember her call sign? Ah, yes. Hello Dewdrop! Can you hear? Felix calling, come here dear.

Sound Effects Cue 28

Lighting Cue 37

(almost before he finishes speaking Dewdrop arrives, entering from the right on an Emmett style machine, part bicycle, part helicopter).
Felix: That was quick.
Dewdrop: *(looking pleased)* Of course. My probationary period is over and I'm now a fully blown fairy, and I've been given my cyclechopper, or hellbike, whichever you like to call it. *(Pats machine)* Isn't she a beauty? Ministry of Magic issue.
Felix: *(puzzled)* But why do you need that complicated machine when you have your own built-in transport —your wings?
Dewdrop: My dear man, fairy wings have been obsolete for donkey's years. We still wear them, of course, because the public likes to think of us in our conventional image, but we rarely use them. The Ministry of Magic boys are very up to date and at one time were thinking of issuing staff with mini cars, but the highways are so frightfully crowded at times, and so are the skyways. Then someone came up with the idea of a two-way vehicle which both flies and trundles, whichever is most suitable at the time.
Felix: Very practical. Now I want some practical help. Have you seen or heard anything of Sally?
Dewdrop: Oh, yes. I saw her a few moments ago. I expect she's wondering what hit her. *(Pats black bag and smiles her satisfaction).*
Felix: If Discord's harmed one hair of her head . . . .

ACT THREE   THE HAPPY WIZARD

Dewdrop: Calm down, calm down, no one has hurt her. As a matter of fact she is very well apart from a little confusion and depression. All perfectly natural and only to be expected in the circumstances. (*Pats bag once more*).

Felix: But if you know where she is why didn't you rescue her? You have the power. Do you mean to say you actually saw her and did . . . .

Dewdrop: Why should I do your work for you? That's the trouble with the young men of today, they expect to have everything done for them without making any effort to help themselves.

Felix: Nothing would give me greater satisfaction than to rescue Sally myself. Where is she?

Dewdrop: There's no point in my telling you because she will no longer be there. Discord is on the move all the time, but no doubt your opportunity will come and in the meantime look for the silver lining, keep your sunny side up and you will come smiling through.

Felix: Is that all the guidance you can give me?

Dewdrop: It's enough. Cheer up! It will all come right in the end. It's in the bag. (*Pats her bag and remounts, makes a wobbly circle of the stage and rides out right*).

Felix: I wish I could share her optimism. Even supposing I were to vanquish Discord, find Harmony and rescue the girls there is still no guarantee that Sally will change her attitude towards me. I doubt if I will ever be able to convince her of my sincerity: every time I open my big mouth I tend to put my foot in it as the saying goes.

Music Cue 27

Even in the Realm of Music it is doubtful if I can hit the right note. (*Sits on upturned drum and reflects*).

Music Cue 28

IF I COULD WRITE MUSIC

Refrain: If I could write music like Gershwin
And magical lyrics like Berlin,
Or were I Hans May
I would soon find a way
Of saying, my darling, I love you.

> To tell of my heart's love I've long tried,
> But when you are near me I'm tongue tied,
> And though I scheme long
> To dream up a theme song
> The words and the music don't ring true.
>
> Rogers and Hammerstein
> Expertly say 'be mine',
> But I know I'll never learn
> The secrets of Jerome Kern.
>
> For I'm just a poor punchinello
> And lacking the touch of Novello,
> So I try in vain
> To compose a refrain
> Just telling you, darling, I love you.
>
> (*verse*) (*recitative*) A night in June, the scene is set
> With shining moon above,
> But I'm so inarticulate
> Concerning talk of love.
> For I'm no strolling troubadour
> With eager serenade,
> When I express my thoughts in song
> I never make the grade.

Felix: (*ruefully*) Singing about the situation only seems to make it worse. (*Footsteps*) Someone's coming. I'll take cover for if it's Discord I stand a better chance if I can take him by surprise. (*Hides behind kiosk*). (*Discord enters left holding Sally and Penny on each arm*).

Discord: Come ladies, it is no use your trying to struggle as I am twice as strong as the two of you together. Besides, struggling is a little undignified, don't you think?

Sally: Where are you taking us?

Discord: If you are thinking to get a message to your mortal friends to come to your rescue, you can forget it. We are going to my lair in the depths of the Purple Mountains, whence no mortal can penetrate without my foreknowledge.

ACT THREE　　　THE HAPPY WIZARD

Penny: The noble Archduke will come to our rescue. He be very clever and full of book learning and will know exactly what to do.

Discord: That wretched, cowering little book worm? I doubt it.

Sally: King Felix will seek you out.

Discord: Your future uncle? I think not. That young man is all bark and no bite!

Felix: (*springs out and confronts Discord*) I venture to contradict you, sir. (*Flings gauntlet in Discord's face and draws sword. The latter relaxes his hold on the women and they break away*). Sally! Penny! Run! Go to Dr. Solfa's library—you will be safe there while I deal with this villain.

Penny: I'll go and get help. (*Goes off but Sally stays, petrified*).

Discord: I accept your challenge. I have taken as much impertinence from you as I can stand. You whippersnapper, you! En garde!

Lighting Cue 38

(*They fight. Felix appears to be the more accomplished swordsman, but he trips and falls. Discord strikes Felix' sword from his hand and stands over his victim*).

Lighting Cue 39

Discord: And so, once high and mighty king, you now come to the moment of truth. I do dislike killing, but now I have no option. But I am a humane demon, my sword is very keen and when I administer the coup de grâce it will be swift and painless. (*Turns to panic stricken Sally*). Now, my dear, this will not be a pretty sight for a young lady to witness, so I suggest you join your aunt, in the library, or wherever it is she was told to go.

Sally: (*Flings herself at Discord's feet*). No! Please do not kill him. Take my life instead.

Discord: My dear young lady, of what use would your life be to me? No more heroics now. Get up and go and find your auntie while I deal with this pestilent young man. He cannot be allowed to live to plague me again.

Sound Effects Cue 29

(*Pushes Sally aside and raises his sword on high. As he is about to strike a clock is heard to chime five*).
Foiled again! (*Sheathes sword*). Well, young man, you can thank your lucky stars you have been saved by the bell. We will resume where we left off, tomorrow. (*Starts to move away left*).

Felix: (*sitting up*) Then you are not going to kill me?
Discord: Not today. It's five o'clock. My hours are nine to five so you will have to wait until tomorrow morning. (*Exit left*).

Lighting Cue 40
Sound Effects Cue 30

Sally: (*going to Felix*) Are you hurt?
Felix: (*in tight lipped anger*) I will live to fight another day —thanks to you.
Sally: You are very ungracious.
Felix: What do you expect? I am in the invidious position of being totally indebted to you and I find it humiliating. Had it not been for your untimely intervention Discord would have executed me, (there would just have been time) and I think I would have preferred it that way.
Sally: That is absurd. You now have another chance.
Felix: A chance which is likely to end in ignominy again. I can't live any longer with failure, Sally. Six days ago I left my country to prove myself; to fight dragons; perform heroic deeds; to be a modern St. George. Why did you have to interfere. It cost me my honour.
Sally: I'll tell you if you will give me a chance. And don't bother any more about St. George, he's been demoted by the Vatican.
Now this is rather difficult to put into words, but I tried to save your life because to me you are the most wonderful person in the world. Don't look so surprised. I did not realise it until you were in mortal peril, but then I knew, and I had to do something, anything to save you: my life would be meaningless if you were dead, although I can expect no more than formal acknowledgement and courtesy from my king.

ACT THREE   THE HAPPY WIZARD

Felix: Sally, do you know what you are saying?
Sally: I am sorry to cause you embarrassment, but under the stress of the last few minutes I just blurted out the truth. (*Turns away*).
Felix: (*turns her round to face him*) You have not embarrassed me, not in the way you think. King I may be, but I am not worthy of sentiments such as yours. The events of the last few days have proved me to be a pretty poor sort of character, a non-hero, in fact.
Sally: But it is not given to everyone to be a public hero even though he may have heroic potential. Opportunity plays such an enormous part in life, and the luck of being in the right place at the right time. But, sire, the days of the great warrior kings are over; once conquered territories are now independent and conquest is an old fashioned word.
Felix: Maybe you are right. But what is there left for me to do to prove myself worthy of controlling the destiny of my people?
Sally: Do you really feel you have to do anything?
Felix: Yes, for their sake and mine.
Sally: I know that time will prove you to be a good king. This excursion outside your own kingdom will be worthwhile, whatever the outcome. You have mixed with ordinary people and the experience will give you greater insight into the lives of your own subjects. In time you will be a kind and democratic monarch, a wise ruler and a friend of his people. A new style monarch.
Felix: (*gravely*) That would be possible only if I had a beautiful and sagacious queen. Will you be my help meet, Sally?
Sally: (*standing back*) I? A peasant, a Pantomaniac? What would the Queen Mother have to say?
Felix: The matter does not concern my mother. I choose my own wife.
Sally: (*carefully*) I have often heard it said that Queen Tryphena is the real power behind the throne.
Felix: Do you really believe that? It's not true. (*Smiles*) My mother is a strong character and is often misjudged. Her life has been by no means easy; she was left a young widow with an infant son and not only did she have to be both mother and father to him, but also the ruler of his country until he came of age.

	When the time came it was no simple task to relinquish the reins suddenly. So, in small matters only I allow her to have her own way. It harms no one, but now I understand how it has given substance to rumours that I am still tied to her apron strings. But let me set your fears at rest—I know she will be delighted with our engagement. After all you are a Pantomaniac and our marriage will mean a reunification of our two countries, in perpetuity.
Sally:	(*slightly annoyed*) You are taking far too much for granted, your Majesty. I have not said I will be a party to any political alliance. I am not sure that I care for marriages of convenience.

Lighting Cue 41

Felix:	(*also slightly annoyed*). I am not suggesting a marriage of convenience. The political angle is just coincidental. Sally, are you being provocative again? Are you playing hard to get?
Sally:	If you think that you are more stupid and bigheaded than I thought you were. Don't you realise that before accepting a proposal a girl expects her suitor to tell her he loves her.
Felix:	(*slightly perplexed*) I assumed you would know that.

Lighting Cue 42

Sally:	I did—but I wanted you to tell me.
Felix:	Here we go again. Will we always argue, Sally? I suppose we will, but it is rather fun. Now seriously, I love you. Will you marry me?

Lighting Cue 43

Sally:	Yes, please. (*He kisses her and the stage is illuminated with a shimmering rose coloured mist as the gauzes are lifted revealing the original row of books. Hilarius, Augustus and Penny enter chattering excitedly*).
Hilarius:	(*bounding forward*) My kingdom, my kingdom, it's here! Thank you, Felix, for finding it for me. Thank you, thank you, thank you. Goodness me, I'm tickled pink, no picked tink. I am so happy, so happy.
Felix:	But I haven't done anything.
Hilarius:	But you have. You have found the final key. The key to love. One look at you and it's quite obvious.

ACT THREE   THE HAPPY WIZARD

Felix: But it was Sally who gave me the key to her heart.
Augustus: The question of responsibility for the success is not important. What is of consequence is that Harmony is found and good would appear to have triumphed over evil.
Felix: Hardly. We have come to some kind of compromise, which is more usual in life. And perhaps that is the moral of our own particular story.
Sally: (*dashing over to Penny*) Aunt Penny, dear, I have some news for you.
Penny: I can guess what it be.
Sally: Not this news.
Penny: (*hugging her*) One look at your face be enough to tell me and I am that glad. It be about you and the king.
Sally: We are going to be married.
Penny: Congratulations, my dears. (*Curtsies to Felix, who takes her hand and kisses it*).
Felix: Thank you, Aunt Penny.
Penny: (*in confusion*) Oh me, Oh my! Fancy being the king's auntie.
Augustus: Congratulations, Sire. (*To Sally*) Felicitations, Ma'am.
Sally: (*extending her hand in the manner born*) We thank you for your good wishes, my dear Archduke (*turns to Felix*). Did I do that correctly?
Felix: Perfectly, my dear.
Sally: (*reverting to her usual manner*) Aunt Penny, when are you and Augustus getting married? Our wedding days must not clash.
Penny: We aren't. We talked it over in Dr. Solfa's library, Gussie and me, and we decided that we were too set in our ways to change. So we are just good friends. After all, I be a career woman and it be too late to alter now.
Sally: But you have sold the tea garden.
Penny: I know, but I have Nelly to think of now. With her co-operation I be intending to open a riding school, specialising in that there show jumping business. And one day I might even hold a royal warrant. I can see it now—Miss Penelope Bunn, Mistress of Equitation to the children of the royal family, by appointment.
Augustus: My dear Miss Bunn, there are no minors in the royal family.

Sally: One day there may be two little princes each as handsome as their royal father.

Felix: And a little princess *almost* as lovely as her mother, the queen.
But all that is in the future. Now what are your plans, Augustus?

Augustus: I shall buy a small place in the country and work on my memoirs. Writing one's autobiography is a fashionable occupation, almost a way of life, and a very lucrative source of income.

Felix: Then everything seems to be settled most satisfactorily.

Sound Effects Cue 31

(There is a sound of bicycle bells ringing and Dewdrop enters right on her machine).

Dewdrop: *(breathless)* Your Majesty, I have a confession. I cannot endure it on my conscience any longer.

Hilarius: Trust a female fairy to want to tell all. No Dewdrop, bliss is ignorance in this particular matter.

Dewdrop: This has nothing to do with the treatment of my two former patients, this is entirely different. I don't know how to begin.

Felix: Cough it up, there's a good girl. You will feel much better after.

Dewdrop: Your Majesty, when I saw how affairs were progressing between you and Sally I took it upon myself to go on ahead and advise the Queen Mother of your impending betrothal so that she would have time to make all the necessary arrangements.

Felix: That was very thoughtful, although I should have preferred to break the news myself. But how did she take it?

Dewdrop: Very well, but that was after . . . .

Augustus: Go on, proceed.

Dewdrop: Well, while I was sitting in the ante chamber, waiting to be received, I hadn't anything else with which to occupy myself, so I spent the time checking my equipment. I was examining my injection gun and—I don't know how to tell you this . . . . the doors to the audience chamber were flung open and it—went—off! *(Pause)* The Queen Mother was standing right in the path of the dart.

ACT THREE   THE HAPPY WIZARD

Felix: You shot my mother?
Augustus: This is high treason and the crime carries the penalty of death. (*Takes off hat and holds it solemnly against his chest. He bows his head*).
Dewdrop: She's not hurt. It was only a medicated dart.
Felix: Thank goodness!
Dewdrop: But . . . but you will find her changed.
Augustus: The effect will be temporary? I trust the dear Queen (*bows*) will soon be herself again?

Sound Effects Cue 32

Dewdrop: Nnnnnnnno! (*Sound of distant fanfare*). Oh dear! Her herald has been hard on my heels all the way from the palace with a proclamation.

Sound Effects Cue 33

(*loud fanfare, the book cover opens and out steps the Queen Mother's Herald*).
Herald: Oyez, oyez, oyez! (*the land of Music people enter from the left and the Pantomaniacs from the right*). Oyez, oyez, oyez!
Hear ye, loyal citizens of Mythuania, Pantomania and all dominions and colonies this proclamation of her Imperial Majesty, the Dowager Queen Tryphena.

> It is with great delight
> We do graciously invite
> All subjects everyone
> To the nuptials of our son
> King Felix with the maiden, Sarah Lunn.
> To bride so prepossessing
> We herewith give our blessing,
> For this match doth reunite
> In alliance infinite
> This realm with Pantomania as one.
> And now we take great pleasure
> In stating further measure
> Intended by our person.
> So hear ye this diversion
> Of our future purpose and inversion.
> It is our firm contention
> (for reasons best not mention)
> That should a younger consort queen
> Venture on the kitchen scene

Domestic strife could not be overcome.
So 'tis our royal intention
To retire from public life (on pension).
Forthwith we'll leave the palace
And thence to our fortalice
Twenty leagues ride upon our pêcheron,
And there, at our country seat
Spend our days in quiet retreat.
With troubles mostly mended
And cares of state now ended
We thankfully conclude our work is done.
Let it now be understood
Marriage is a likelihood,
We intend to take a spouse
(trained of course, around the house)
For now's the time to eschew widowhood.
The chosen man to share our nook
Is Augustus, good Archduke
And companion to our well loved son.
But should he dare our suit to mock
His head will roll upon the block
For spurning of our hand is just not done.
In accordance with our royal wishes, today
will be a public holiday.

Here ends our proclamation!
(fanfare and Herald re-enters book. There is reaction from the crowd and Augustus falls to his knees and Felix helps him rise).

Felix: Don't be afraid, Augustus, you don't have to comply with this. As the sovereign, I will rescind any order of execution my mother may issue.

Augustus: There will be no need for that, your majesty. It is an honour, a privilege ....

Felix: Then you mean to go through with this shot gun marriage? There is no need.

Augustus: I do not see it thus. It has always been my great pleasure to try and gratify Her Majesty's *(bows)* slightest whim, but this command to be the royal lady's *(bows)* consort is the supreme honour and in late middle age I find it almost overwhelming.

Felix: You may well find it so! But if you are sure this is the right course for you, then accept my sincere congratulations .... Dad!

ACT THREE   THE HAPPY WIZARD

Penny: Now isn't this nice. Your Majesty will have a lovely stepfather and I be sure Gussie, I mean His Grace the Archduke will make a wonderful husband for Queen Tryphena. Everything seems to be too good to be true. Mr. Wizard?
Hilarius: Yes, Miss Penny?
Penny: Look on the last page in the book and find out if there really is going to be a happy ending. I don't trust that nasty demon not to put a spoke in the wheel at the last moment.

Sound Effects Cue 34

Lighting Cue 44

(*There is a flash, a roll of thunder and Discord appears left, spotlighted in green*).

Discord: How right you are, dear lady. But no doubt there will be plenty of helpers to pull it out. But believe me (*complacently*) you cannot do without old Discord. I provide the shadows to contrast with the sunshine, the troubles, out of which happiness often comes, and the deterrents from which often springs success. I provide the spur, the incentive without which life would be very dull. I am the fairy of divine discontent.
Dewdrop: You are moralising and that's my prerogative!

Lighting Cue 45

Hilarius: (*coming centre stage*) Now Coughdrop, now Wallyscag, er Scallywag. A temporary truce, if you please, while I do as Miss Bunn requested. (*Goes to book and peers round cover*).

Music Cue 29

It says 'and they all lived happily ever after for ever and a day'. Now isn't that nice?
(*the company link arms, Hilarius in the centre, Penny and Augustus on one side and Felix and Sally on the other and to a reprise of Sally's music they sing:—*)

Music Cue 30

Lighting Cue 46

There'll be a happy ending
With gladness
Transcending
All our sighs.

There'll be a happy meeting
With gay words
Of greeting
No good-byes.

And now that fate has intervened
Our troubles soon will mend
Happily our tale will have the
Old traditional end.

There'll be a bright tomorrow
No sadness,
No sorrow
No grey skies.

A happy ever after
With joy and
With laughter
And blue skies.

Music Cue 31

(*the music changes to 'Back in the Book' and two by two the company re-enters the book until only Hilarius is left alone singing the final verse*).

Hilarius: Back to our tome,
No more to roam.
We wish you good night and a safe
Journey home.

(*he disappears into the book only to emerge a second later with two milk bottles and a stuffed black cat which he places outside. He goes into the book and closes the cover*).

FINAL CURTAIN

Lighting Cue 47

Music Cue 32

PRODUCTION NOTES

STYLE OF PRESENTATION.

The general style of performance may be summed up in two words—pace and panache!

Dialogue, particularly in the early scenes needs a lively tempo and actors must be quick in taking up their cues: gestures should be bold and manners a little extravagant, after all this is a fairy tale, albeit a modern one.

However, in fairy tale tradition, Dewdrop and Discord as the personification of good and evil make all their entrances and exits from right and left respectively and as far as the confines of the set allow do not cross over into one another's territory.

Sloppy sentimentality should be avoided in the love scenes between Felix and Sally. In general the approach is light, emphasis being given to the gaiety and diversion of the game of falling in love. In Act III, however, despite the badinage it is essential that the feeling of sincerity between these two is put across with conviction.

Apart from the small amount of by-play between Penelope and Nelly at the end of Act II and the mock duel between Augustus and Discord any further slapstick is unnecessary and out of place.

With the exception of 'Back in the Book' and 'No Happy Ending' the other musical numbers may be omitted although their inclusion does add colour to the production. A few simple dance steps introduced into the 'Back in the Book' number improves its effect, but unless there are talented dancers in the company the insertion of other routines is not necessary. If a drummer is available to back up the pianist this adds considerably to the musical impact.

This is escaptist entertainment for both adults and children and therefore the production should be as diverting and colourful as posible, with the accent on gentle satire.

CHARACTERS.

There are seven speaking parts for men and five for women, but if necessary the parts of Daffy and Melody and Billy and Dr. Solfa may be doubled. Nelly, of course, may be played by two members of either sex or one of each unless a real live pony is available! The Herald (at the end of Act III) may also be doubled with either end of Nelly.

During the Proclamation in Act 1 scene 2 several extras may be brought on as a village crowd but this is not essential; in the same way during the scene in the Realm of Music extras may be used.

Felix is about 25-30, attractive and slightly arrogant, he sees himself as a dashing hero, but gradually matures under Sally's influence, realising that despite his exalted rank he is but an ordinary young man.

Augustus should be a complete contrast to Felix. Middle aged, fairly short in stature, pedantic and prim. Although not afraid of administering a tutorial reproof to his royal master he stands in great awe of the unseen Queen Mother and is terrified of physical danger.

Hilarius is elderly but *active*. He should *not* be portrayed as bent double and suffering from ague, but as a sprightly, delightfully vague and slightly mischievous old man. It does not matter whether he is tall and thin or short and plump.

Discord must be well built, flamboyant and noisy; an obvious but likeable rogue.

Penelope is a happy character with a countrywoman's simple dignity and this must not be spoiled by a 'pantomime dame' interpretation. She is middle aged and pleasant looking, speaking with a faint Mummerset accent.

Dewdrop although dressed in the shimmering white of tradition there is nothing of the conventional sprite about this fairy. Her manner varies between that of the earnest student and the pseudo cheerfulness of the stage district nurse.

Daffy is a not-so-simple village maiden determined to get her man.

Billy a mono-syllabic talker who manages to put a wealth of meaning into his utterances and ejaculations. Again, a not-so-simple yokel.

Sally despite her simple background looks every inch a heroine albeit one with radical ideas. A very practical young woman who sometimes tries to hide her true feelings under a slightly off hand manner.

Nelly a nightmare of a quadruped. The part(s) should be played down, rather than over-played.

Dr. Solfa A maestro, a showman type. A suspicion of an Italian accent is an asset.

Melody a nice, refined lady! Old fashioned and wallowing in nostalgia.

Herald (One appearance only, at the end of the play). He must have a powerful, declamatory voice and a definite presence.

SETTINGS.

These may be simple, making use of cut-outs against a cyclorama or curtains if flats are not available.

The opening scene of the play takes place on the first third of the stage thus enabling the bulk of scene two to be set up behind the book screen. The end of Act I scene 2 makes a natural break during which interval the set for Act II may be erected, and again the end of Act II indicates another natural break—this time for a shorter interval when Act III may be set up. It should be noted that the gate and the kiosk used at the beginning of this Act should be well in towards the wings so that when the gauze curtain is either flown or drawn the former do not detract from the book screen.

COSTUMES.

A costume plot is given on page 99, but this is only an indication of possible designs. It is suggested that the costumes of the various pairs, i.e., Felix and Sally, Augustus and Penelope, etc., are in similar colours but this is not essential. Make up, with the exception of Discord, whose appearance may verge on the fantastic, is straightforward.

FURNITURE AND PROPERTIES,

A list of these is given on page 100. All these are easily obtained and Dewdrop's Hellibike can be adapted from an ordinary bicycle to which is fixed the frame of a golfing umbrella plus as many 'Heath Robinson' and 'Roland Emett' type of gadgets as the producer thinks necessary.

LIGHTING.

A lighting plot appears on page 102. It is not always necessary to herald Discord's entrances or exits with a flash of lightning, particularly when he enters in disguise. A green spot could be used as an alternative, in which case the rolls of thunder detailed in the sound effects plot should be omitted.

MUSIC.

A detailed music plot is on page 103.

SOUND EFFECTS.

Full details are shown on page 105. The harp cadenza accompanying Dewdrop's entrances and exits is optional.

COSTUME PLOT

Felix — Throughout the play. Royal blue cloak edged with wide gold braid and lined with white. Blue dagged tunic and hose, white fullsleeved shirt. Sword belt. Fairly simple gilded crown (the latter not worn after scene 1).

Augustus — Throughout the play. Maroon tunic (longer than Felix's), hose, cloak and hat with liripipe.

Hilarius — Costume throughout the play. Voluminous midnight blue robe patterned with stars and moons. There must be a pocket in the robe. Long white beard and round spectacles which he wears on the end of his nose.
Act I scene 1. As above but with black bowler hat, thereafter with pointed steeple hat.

Discord — Act I scene 1. Dark green sequin embroidered tunic, dark green hose, Burgundian style cap, sword belt.
Act I scene 1. Voluminous Middle Eastern type robe and embroidered fez.
Act I scene 2. Original dark green costume over which is worn a richly embroidered tabard in the royal colours (blue, silver, white and gold) with a herald's cap. No sword belt.
Act II. Original costume over which is worn silver breastplate, gauntlets and helmet with plume.
Act III scene 1. As above.
Act III (final entrance). As for the first entrance in Act I scene 1.

Penelope — Throughout the play. Maroon and white long dress. White wimple.

Dewdrop — White tutu and sparkling tiara worn throughout the play plus college scarf and spectacles for first entrance only.

Billy — Throughout. Holland smock type tunic and yellow leggings. Battered yellow hat with upturned brim and bedraggled green feather.

Daffy — Throughout. Yellow dress beneath which are three petticoats (1) green (2) orange (3) white. White apron and kerchief.

Sally — Throughout. A long simple royal blue dress, hanging sleeves lined with white. A plain girdle round the waist. No head-dress, but her hair may be caught back with a ribbon.

Dr. Solfa Black short tunic appliqued with silver 'note' motifs, white hose. Academic cap and gown.
Melody Long lavender gown, steeple henin with flowing pale grey veil.
The Revolutionary (non-speaking walk-on part). Long black cloak, black slouch hat.
Herald
Dark hose, tabard similar to that worn by Discord in Act 1 scene 2. Hat (can be same one as worn by Discord).

FURNITURE AND PROPERTY PLOT
Act I

Scene 1
Book screen.
Fly leaf of centre book behind practical door.
Stacks of outsize books down stage R. and L.
Cloak—(Felix).
Sword do.
Crown do.
Bowler hat (Hilarius).
Umbrella do.
Notebook do.
Sword—(Discord).
Roll of Carpet—(Discord—2nd entrance).
Wand—(Dewdrop).
Black bag containing:—Wizard's tall hat and wand, delivery note and pencil (Dewdrop).
Wooden clothes horse (offstage L.).

End of scene
Strike Book screen, piles of books and any other props.

Scene 2
The cottage, chestnut tree, bushes with some detachable leaves, rustic bench already set up behind book screen. Set small tables and stools (number to be decided according to size of stage), bottle of wine on table, also salt, pepper and mustard pots, sugar bowl.
Offstage—
Pile folded table clothes—(Sally).
Box cutlery   do.

Notebook and pencil (Daffy).
Tray with soup bowls, one containing dish cloth.
Billy—(Daffy).
Wand—(Hilarius).
3 mugs—(Billy).
Trumpet—(Discord).
2 silver keys—dropped from flies.
Small bag containing coins—(Augustus).
Cloak—(Felix).
Bag containing:—2 aerosols, casette and gun—(Dewdrop).
Quill pen—(Hilarius).
Lunch basket—(Billy).

End of Act

    Strike set and all props.

ACT II

Scene 1

Set mill, groundrow, bank rostrum with artificial grass covering plus loose lump of turf and tree cut outs.
Black bag with contents as in previous scene (Dewdrop).
Felix's cloak (Sally).
Carrot on stick—(Penny).
Wand   do.
Offstage—Box on wheels containing::—saucepan, dustbin lid, tray with straps attached, oven gloves, feather duster, toasting fork—(Nelly).
Sword—(Discord).
Sword—(Felix).
Garter—(Penny).
Black bag plus out size hypodermic, box of pills, peppermint lump, two keys with ribbon attached.
Another key (dropped from flies).
Paper back copy of 'The Happy Wizard' (Felix).

End of Act.

    Strike set and all props.

ACT III

Scene 1

Set book screen (behind gauze). Set gate plus bell, kiosk and drums.
Sword—(Felix).

Baton—(Solfa).
Smoking bomb—(Revolutionary).
Bicycle (Dewdrop).
Black bag   do.
Gauntlets—(Felix).
Sword—(Discord).
2 milk bottles and stuffed black cat—(Hilarius).

LIGHTING PLOT

1. House lights to half.
2. End of Overture—fade house lights out.
3. On curtain up bring up acting area lights to half—spotlight on centre book cover.
4. After Augustus's entrance fade spot on book cover and bring up acting area lights to full.
5. Fade acting area lights to half at the same time bring up spot on book as Augustus says 'The Queen Mother would no doubt . . . '
6. Fade spot on book and bring up acting area lights to full on Felix's line 'Your pet dragon?'
7. Lightning flash after Felix's line 'Where is he to be found?'
8. Lightning flash on Discord's line ' I will be back'.
9. Bring up spot on book cover on first few bars of 'Back in the Book'.
10. Fade spot after Penelope's entrance.
11. Bring up green spot on Discord—at end of line 'Let's see what we'll see'.
12. Fade green spot on 'Pray be not alarmed'.
13. Lightning flash on Discord's exit.
14. End of scene 1 fade to blackout as quartet exeunt.
15. Scene 2 bring up full stage daylight lighting.
16. Lightning flash as Discord exits.
17. Start to fade daylight lighting on 'Dotty old man'. This must be very gradual.
18. Start to bring up sunset lighting on 'No coach, no Augustus'.
19. Fade to blackout on 'Tally-ho! We're off!'
20. House lights up when curtain down.
21. House lights to half on commencement of entracte.
22. House lights out as entracte finishes.

ACT II

23. Bring up sunset lighting.
24. At the same time light up owls' eyes.
25. Start gradually dimming sunset and bringing up moonlight on acting area.
26. Start increasing moonlight on Daffy and Billy's entrance bringing it up to full on their exit. Hold.
27. Lightning flash on line 'Conditions no longer apply'.
28. Bring up general lighting on Nelly's entrance with box of Equipment. Hold until Discord's exit with Penny and Sally.
29. Lightning flash on Discord's exit.
30. Fade to blackout as Felix, Augustus and Hilarius go out.
31. House lights up on curtain.
32. House lights to half on commencement of entracte.
33. House lights out at finish of entracte.

ACT III

34. Bring up full stage lighting on acting area.
35. Gradually start dimming lights—bringing down to half by
36. the time Felix says 'How dark it grows' then hold.
37. Start to bring up lighting on Dewdrop's entrance on bicycle.
38. Spotlight on Felix and Discord during duel.
39. Fade spot as Felix falls and bring up general lighting in acting area to full.
40. Lightning flash on Discord's exit.
41. Start fading general lighting on Felix's line 'I am not suggesting a marriage of convenience'.
42. Start bringing up rose lighting on 'I assumed you would know that'.
43. Bring up rose lighting to full ..
44. Lightning flash on 'spoke in the wheel at the last moment'.
45. Bring up spotlight on book on 'Now Coughdrop—now Wallyscag—'
46. Full stage lighting for finale 'There'll be a Happy Ending'.
47. House lights up after final curtain.

MUSIC PLOT
ACT I

1. Overture.
2. Curtain up. A few bars of 'Back in the Book' fading as door begins to move.
3. Intro. 'Back in the Book'.
4. Song. 'Back in the Book'.

5. Reprise of 'Back in the Book'. One verse to be sung then continue with music only until curtain up on scene two.
6. Opening of scene 2. Start fading music, ending as Daffy starts speaking.
7. Intro. 'Dreaming Dreams'.
8. Song. 'Dreaming Dreams'.
9. Intro. Reprise of 'Back in the Book'.
10. Song. 'Back in the Book' (new verses).
11. Intro. 'The Mixture'.
12. Song. 'The Mixture'.
13. Intro. 'Giddy-yup Nelly'.
14. Song: 'Giddy-yup Nelly'.
15. Entracte. 'Back in the Book' fading into 'Dreaming Dreams'.

ACT II

16. Opening of Act II fade 'Dreaming Dreams' into 'The Mixture' on Hilarius' entrance, ending as he takes up the melody.
17. Intro. 'Breath of Fresh Air'.
18. Song. 'Breath of Fresh Air'.
19. Intro. 'No Happy Ending'.
20. Song. 'No Happy Ending'.
21. Reprise (music only) 'Breath of Fresh Air' played slowly throughout duel but speeding up as necessary towards the end.
22. Cue 21 ends.
23. Reprise of 'Back in the Book' (music only) finishing just after curtain falls.

ACT III

24. Entracte. 'Back in the Book' fading into 'No Happy Ending'.
25. Opening of Act III. Fade music as Felix begins speaking.
26. A few bars of Chopin's 'Revolutionary' fading on Revolutionary's exit.
27. Intro. 'If I Could Write Music'.
28. Song. 'If I Could Write Music'.
29. Intro of reprise of 'No Happy Ending'.
30. Song 'No Happy Ending' (new verses).
31. Music of 'No Happy Ending' changes to 'Back in the Book' and continues until final curtain.
32. Play out to Overture.

SOUND AND EFFECTS PLOT
ACT I
Scene 1
1. Start smoke on Agustus' line 'Come off it indeed' and continue until Hilarius enters.
2. Start roaring just after smoke begins and continue as above.
3. Fade Smoke. Cue one ends.
4. Cue 2 ends.
5. Roll of thunder immediately following lightning flash at end of Felix's line 'Where is he to be found?'
6. Roll of thunder immediately following Discord's exit line 'But I will be back'.
7. Thunder following lightning flash after Discord's exit line '—— a wondrous ride; Farewell!'
8. Telephone number unobtainable noise immediately following Hilarius' line 'Wizard calling, please come here'.
9. Telephone ringing tone followed by a harp cadenza on Hilarius' line 'Wizard Calling, please come, dear'.
10. Harp cadenza on Dewdrop's exit line 'Good luck go with you. Farewell!'
11. 'Whinney' at end of Hilarius' line 'Please send horses, one, two, three . . . . . .'

Scene 2
12. Distant fanfare at end of Daffy's line 'Billy, you're wanted'.
13. Loud fanfare at end of Hilarius's line 'Listen!'
14. Thunder clap following lightning flash on Discord's exit line 'Oyez, oyez, oyez'.
15. Harp cadenza at end of Hilarius' line 'I will take it with me when I follow him'.
16. Horses' hooves approaching on Penny's line 'Coach driven by six white horses'.

ACT II
17. Soft 'owl hoots' as curtain opens and during Felix's soliloquy.
18. 'Pop' noise as Dewdrop fires dart—immediately after Sally gives cloak to Felix. This cue will have to be given by some visual signal as there is no appropriate line of dialogue.
19. Second 'pop' on second shot which comes after Dewdrop's line 'missed the vital spot'.
20. Telephone number unobtainable noise right after Hilarius's line 'Wizard calling, come in dear'.
21. Harp cadenza immediately following repeat of above line.

22. Horses' hooves on Felix' line 'If you could only see him'. Continue until Nelly's entrance.
23. Clap of thunder immediately following lightning at end of Felix's line 'Conditions no longer apply'.
24. Horses' hooves during Hilarius's incantation, ceasing on Nelly's entrance.
25. Harp cadenza at end of Hilarius's line 'You must not get dumps in the down'.
26. Harp cadenza on Dewdrop's exit line 'Farewell'.

ACT III

27. Tubular Bell at end of Felix's line 'Thank you for bringing me back to my senses'.
28. Harp cadenza on Dewdrop's entrance.
29. Clock strikes 5 at end of Discord's line 'He cannot be allowed to live to plague me again'.
30. Thunder clap following lightning on Discord's exit.
31. Harp cadenza, followed by bicycle bell and multi-tone horn at end of Felix's line 'settled most satisfactorily'.
32. Distant fanfare at end of Dewdrop's long drawn out Nnnnnnnno!'
33. Louder fanfare after 'proclamation' (Dewdrop's line).
34. Thunder clap following lightning flash on Discord's entrance.

Moderato

BACK IN THE BOOK

(Song No. 1)

Moderato

JUST DREAMING DREAMS

(Song No. 2)

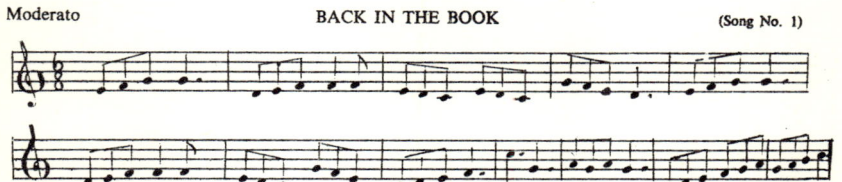

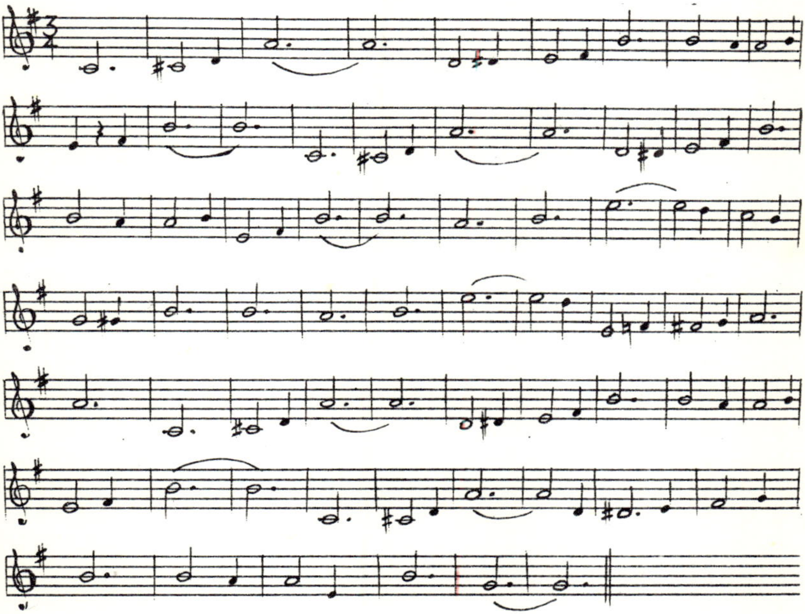

Allegretto THE MIXTURE (Song No. 3)

Moderato

GIDDY-YUP NELLY

(Song No. 4)

Moderato

BREATH OF FRESH AIR

(Song No. 5)

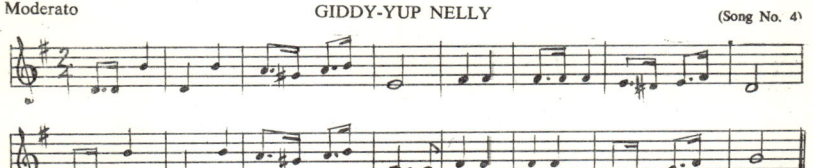

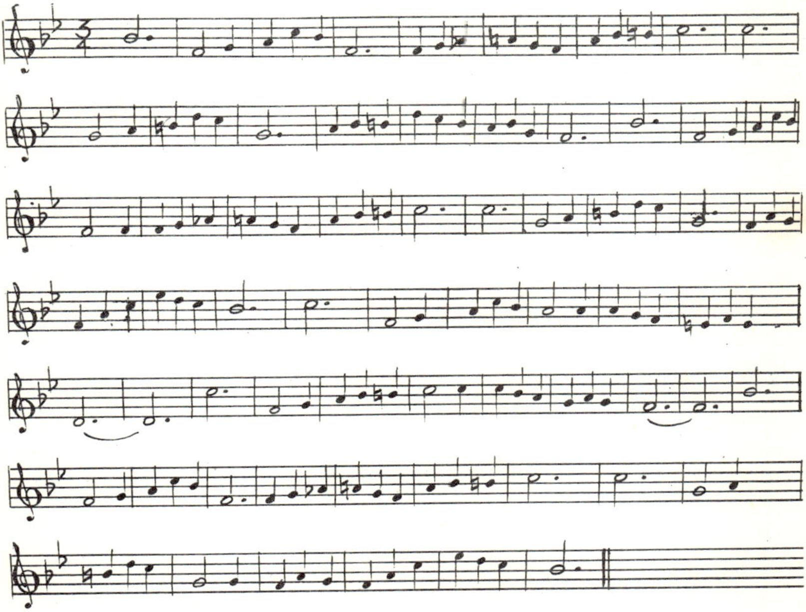

Moderato IF I COULD WRITE MUSIC (Song No. 7)